W9-BNO-300

the artificial white man

Also by Stanley Crouch

Nonfiction

Reconsidering the Souls of Black Folk (with Playthell Benjamin)
One Shot Harris: The Photographs of Charles "Teenie" Harris
Always in Pursuit: Fresh American Perspectives
Notes of a Hanging Judge
The All-American Skin Game, or, The Decoy of Race

Fiction

Don't the Moon Look Lonesome

the artificial white man

essays on authenticity

STANLEY CROUCH

BASIC
CIVITAS
BOOKS

A Member of the Perseus Books Group
New York

Portions of this book originally appeared in the following:

"Baby Boy" appeared as "A Lost Generation and Its Exploiters" in *The New York Times*. Copyright © 2001 by The New York Times Co. Reprinted with permission. "Appetite Is the Main Course" is reprinted from volume 4, number 1 of *Literary Imagination: The Review of the Association of Literary Scholars and Critics*, © 2002. "The Novel as Blues Suite" is reprinted from volume 5, number 1 of *Literary Imagination*, © 2003. Used by permission of the Association of Literary Scholars and Critics. "Don't Be Like Mike" appeared in *The New York Observer*. A portion of "Most Vote for Literary Segregation, Others Don't" first appeared, in slightly different form, in the *Los Angeles Times*.

Books published by BasicCivitas are available at special discounts for bulk purchases in the United States by corporations, institutions, and other organizations. For more information, please contact the Special Markets Department at the Perseus Books Group, 11 Cambridge Center, Cambridge MA 02142, or call (617) 252-5298 or (800) 255-1514, or e-mail special.markets@perseusbooks.com.

Designed by Lisa Kreinbrink

Library of Congress Cataloging-in-Publication Data

Crouch, Stanley.
     The artificial white man : essays on authenticity / Stanley Crouch.
        p. cm.
     Includes index.
     ISBN 0-465-01515-8 (alk. paper)
     1. Race relations in mass media.   2. Mass media—United States.   I. Title.

P94.5.M552U6275 2004
305.8—dc22
                                                                    2004011998

04   05   06 / 10   9   8   7   6   5   4   3   2   1

To my daughter

Contents

the artificial white man

Introduction

Blues to Be Authentic

I gave this volume the title *The Artificial White Man* because it implies the dominant theme: authenticity. Subjects such as Quentin Tarantino, Michael Jackson, John Singleton, Juan Luis Borges, Ernest Hemingway, William Faulkner, Duke Ellington, Saul Bellow, David Shields (the subject of the title essay), Alfred Appel, and contemporary American fiction allow me the necessary opportunities to investigate my subject. Some are celebrated, some are spanked, some are celebrated *and* spanked.

In a number of chapters I attack those who present themselves as authentic or claim to expose the inauthentic while actually pushing forward a high- or low-quality version of counterfeit. But I do not think the reasons for our obsession with authenticity are simple, nor do I misapprehend the complexity of the moment in which we live on this earth. Ours is a technological era that often defines itself and achieves commercial success by continuing to do a better job at making the unreal seem true. Due to the many-layered rebellion against the pervasiveness of the unreal, we live in a period of great disillusionment; as idols

crash, conventions are rejected that upheld various forms of bigotry arriving in the areas of class, ethnicity, religion, color, and
sex. The result is that part of our contemporary national paranoia expresses itself in the belief that someone may have put
something over on us, that we have too often been duped into
believing that the counterfeit is the authentic.

In the bush or somewhere up in somebody's mountains, we
assume—or hope—that there are people whose sense of life
has not been totally encroached on by the boxed, electronic
shadow world of television or the Internet universe in which
cyberspace seems as real to many as God, angels, and heaven
are to an atheist. If that purportedly innocent existence is what
some might consider luck, we haven't had any on this soil in a
very, very long time. There is hardly a space of one hundred
square miles that has not been defined and redefined by the cal-
lous and inspiring nature of modernity.

We have been modern for so long that authenticity is largely
a meaningless term, though there are distinct ethnic styles that
don't quite tell us what we think they do. One reason is that this
nation—long, long ago—switched tracks from the local to the
express. So influences come and go at very high speeds. Traditions are remade and abandoned or reimagined, sometimes for
the better, sometimes—which is where the blues always makes
its move—for the worst. Our country is some kind of a mon-
grel that is spiritually a chameleon but always remains a bastard.
And you can be sure that starting as an American bastard in a
world where former European bastards have family lines long
enough to make them arrogant is another reason why being
authentic might be something of a recurring problem.

Across our democratic vista, for all of its tragic tales, we have
seen that the ultimate truth of humanity is fairly simple: no
qualities of any sort that have to do with intelligence or will or

spirit can be assumed on the basis of our favorite lines of demarcation. Color, sex, religion, class, and point of geographic origin are just more blanks that, even at close range, don't leave powder burns on the target board of Americana. The individual still has to sign on the dotted line for anything to make sense or become specific. (Even though he was not an American, the great Borges, an Argentine, trumped Hemingway in that area of recognition, as I show in "The Novel as Blues Suite.")

The elite version of authenticity used to begin above but now has been discredited. Nothing has survived the holocaust of close, close scrutiny, not government, not business, not religion, not ethnicity, not the upper class, not the family unit, not parenting, not adolescence, not childhood, nothing at all. With the fall of the high, the energy from below has been elevated in our reimagining of traditions. A purity has been projected onto the bottom and that projection has risen to a great influence. Americans now fear, with greater intensity than ever, becoming bloodless, stiff, "uncool." (David Shields is a notable example.) It is very difficult to come in contact with what is considered cool—or achieve the status that comes of surviving the harsher realities of life—if one is born above. The assault on middle-class life in our television shows and our movies allows us to recognize that we are constantly being signaled about authenticity. A blue, despairing cry is coming at us from behind the trends of extreme hairdos, piercings, ethnic getups, aggressively bad taste, nose rings, tattoos, and the fashion collages that draw so badly and so freely from the worlds of the primitive, science fiction, and street gang posturing.

On the lower frequencies of what we call urban America, young men who hope to become hip-hop stars risk imprisonment or death in order to get "street credentials," meaning hoodlum authenticity. So we are now at the place where moving from the inauthentic to the authentic can become a rite of passage allowing a person to become a brand who wears a seal of approval, like the purple stamp on meat that passes inspection.

This book is an argument with all of that, however sympathetic it might be to the search for alternatives to our disappointments. One position it takes is that empty-headed appropriation or assumed membership in a besieged elite, like the "white world," is far different from inspired reactions to influences from outside of one's class and ethnic conventions. It is also true in my mind that ethnic identity, however slippery it can be, should not remove complexity from the natural history of Americana but add *more* distinctions, a greater variety of nuance, some perspectives that allow the insider and the outsider to be seen more clearly. I hope to present, through unsentimental affirmation, a new form of rebellion in our time of cosmetic dissent. While it is obvious that I do not deny the distinct styles of different ethnic groups, I believe that these preoccupations have made it harder for some people to seek their own individuality because they feel that they should follow a recipe for how to be an acceptable member of their ethnic group. This has had a bad effect on our fiction, since there are ethnic characters that too many writers do not feel free enough to try and imagine into their work. (Besides helping give thematic form to the book, this is why William Faulkner and *Go Down, Moses* are referred to more than once.) This gussied-up version of segregation also misses the importance of certain domestic art forms because they have not been seen as authentic high art. It has gotten us into a big, fat, spreading mess, and I hope that this collection gives a sizable helping hand to getting us out of it.

Baby Boy Blues

DIRECTOR AND SCREENWRITER JOHN SINGLETON'S recent *Baby Boy,* which was both loved and hated, arrived at a unique moment in our time. In areas of popular entertainment and even in supposedly serious criticism, the humanity of black people is under attack. It is a period of deep crisis in which nuanced discussion is difficult. Nothing about black Americans can be discussed in a vacuum and little that looks at things seriously can escape the past. The many thousands of bigoted denigrations that went unchallenged for so long can now be used as references to dismiss a work of art—especially if that work is critical of any manifestations in contemporary or traditional Afro-American culture.

When Singleton set out to take a critical look at those strutting young Los Angeles black men who father children by various women and make little or no effort to support them, he was stepping into what has long been a serious mess. Anyone who goes down into the darker ranges of the Afro-American world faces danger, since what one finds down there can so easily be placed within the dead world of the stereotype. In that world, characters exist only as lifeless puppets pulled into action for the perpetuation of poisonous myths about the unchanging essence of a purportedly inferior group.

We see the complexity of the troubles everywhere, with and without black cooperation. Images of black youth seen on MTV, BET, or VH1, as the most obvious examples, are not far removed from those D. W. Griffith used in *Birth of a Nation,* where Reconstruction Negroes were depicted as bullying, hedonistic buffoons ever ready to bloody somebody. This is the new minstrelsy. The neo-Sambo is sturdily placed in our contemporary popular iconography. He can be seen, for instance, mugging or scowling in Trick Daddy's "I'm a Thug," where gold teeth, drop-down pants, and tasteless jewelry abound. Then there is the fast-tailed hussy, rolling her rump at the camera or challenging some anonymous man to satisfy her in Missy's latest. These videos are created primarily for the material enrichment of black entertainers, producers, and directors, not present-day whites, who would be run off the planet if they—like the creators of nineteenth-century minstrelsy—were responsible for the images, the ideas, and the content.

It is against this backdrop of dehumanization that a brave work such as *Baby Boy* must be assessed. On the surface, it seems no more than an exploitation of people who were struggling to find themselves, or had no interest in going beyond where they were, or seemed unconcerned about becoming anything more than what they already were. But what Singleton actually tried to do cannot easily be made light of, particularly since there are so few black films bent on probing serious subjects. That is because black characters, regardless of the color of the screenwriter, rarely exist for artistic purposes. They tend to fulfill some fantasy or some craven attempt to take advantage of the fact that black moviegoers constitute such a large percent-

age of ticket buyers. Such characters are just props, as the writer
Clayton Riley once called them.

Singleton is after more than props. He questions the mores of
his characters and shows young black men caught in ritual
behavior that is about arrested development on one hand and
bitter rage at their limitations on another. They listen to no one,
make no own rules but follow unproductive conventions based
in getting high, impregnating women, and pretending to be in
control of adult or violent worlds that press them to the canvas
at will. At one point, with a tragic depth one would find exceptional in *any* American film, a character prays that he and his
buddy be shown the way but, if they cannot be given a direction,
the young man asks God to "forgive us for being lost."

That sense of life gives the film its depth, its sense of tragedy,
of violence, of murder, of rape, of passing on the bloody gauntlet of abuse, of girls who become mothers before they become
women and struggle with sons who are males but not men. We
see onetime teenage mothers trying to get their grown sons out
of their houses and into lives where personal responsibility is normal, not rare. Singleton gives us men who once followed the dark
tracks of the thug life but finally got themselves together. They
find it almost impossible to explain to these young guys that they
do not have to repeat a stupid cycle in which nothing is proved
and little is learned—other than how dumb the whole hoodlum
stroke was in the first place.

There is even a "Man Who Shot *Liberty Valance*" morality; it
accepts the killing of a young, murderous monster as a harsh
rite of passage. This makes the community a better place to be
by permanently removing one more snake. Though the protagonist—who is traumatized immediately following the murder—
is not haunted by the killing when we last see him, director John
Ford taught us that one day the murder will return to the front

of his brain and he will recall it as the tragic moment when he rose above where he began, when he learned the cost of living among armed young men who use real guns as if they were cap pistols.

Still, a tight focus on such people that did not include a more comprehensive picture of black Los Angeles was seen as having no value in certain quarters. A good number of well-to-do black people considered the film an insult and proof that, as one magazine editor said to me, "John Singleton, with all of his success and his new address among the Hollywood crew, doesn't know any more about those people now than anybody else. He is just as much an outsider. That is why the writer I assigned to do a piece about the film decided not to write anything after a screening. It was a waste of time on something as worthless as that."

Others thought the film was pornographic. They did not recognize that the erotic scenes—unlike sexual minstrelsy—reveal aspects of the psychological identities of the participants, making them much more than bodies performing intimate acts. The scenes can trick us into believing that as long as a guy from that background can erotically satisfy a gal he has mistreated, his transgressions will be forgiven. One unexpected scene takes place when the major character—who is a *true* hound—discovers, almost in the middle of the act, that he does not want to have sex with anyone other than the young woman who has paid her dues to win his faithfulness. Singleton even has a moment when a single mother is about to be raped but the presence of her protesting infant son elicits unexpected compassion from the rapist. Determined not to let his thug mask drop, he calls the child a dirty name and storms off.

Those are the kinds of things that make *Baby Boy* special. Its shortcomings begin in the beginning, when a discussion of black male behavior is heard in a voice-over. The words are from Francis Cress Welsing, an intellectual buffoon of the first order, whose color theories almost justify the term "reverse racism." Her thoughts, taken from the dubious *Isis Papers,* explain how black males can be infantilized by a racist society. This is pushed home by the image of the lead, pop singer and model Tyrese Gibson, fully grown but still in the womb. Some of the cutting seems clumsy and there is a secondary tale about a brother who was murdered that is never made clear. With a picture of Tupac Shakur overlooking the bedroom of the lead character, Singleton makes clear what the best of our black filmmakers have been saying for quite some time—those who model themselves on the thug life advocated by the Shakurs become dangerous not only to themselves but to everyone else. This is far beyond a racial point because it speaks to codes of living, which are always the subjects of comprehensive narrative art.

Baby Boy therefore stands tall in times like these and makes a very strong third part of the trilogy Singleton began with his first film, *Boyz in the Hood* (1991). In that first effort, Singleton went far beyond the skin-deep renditions of certain segments of black youth and their troubles on the street. Without its success, it is hard to imagine *Menace II Society* getting financing and going on to establish directors Allen and Albert Hughes as hot talents who could bring humanity to people so easily reduced to cartoonish, amoral miscreants in other popular contexts.

There are other problems that Singleton has to face because he, like every serious black creator in every arena, has to address the fact that there is a large black audience for the kind of drivel that so many others protest. It is not as though the new minstrelsy does not have black followers, legions of them. When his finest work thus far, *Rosewood,* was released, the empty-headed *Booty Call* came out and took the money off the table.

Rosewood was a major American film because it, on an epic scale, moved the Afro-American experience into the mythic arenas in which John Ford cast his work, where the real and the mythological stood together, where authenticity and poetic exaggeration reinforced each other, where real characters and archetypes spoke to one another and worked together. Never, in the history of American film, had southern racist hysteria been shown so clearly. Color, class, and sex were woven together on a level that Faulkner would have appreciated. For once, the parallels between Afro-American and European Jewish experience, so often cited but so clumsily discussed, were brought home. We saw different levels and degrees of racism as Singleton got his white actors to become people, not symbols. There was also a staggering rendition of how one act of dishonesty, in a moment of near madness, could bring down a holocaust rooted in envy and resentment. It was a high point in contemporary cinema.

Rosewood showed us what John Singleton can do when he has the freedom to fully explore his talents and the identification and alienation that continue to tie our society in knots. Someday we may see someone carry through what Spike Lee attempted in *Bamboozled,* which shows the close alignment between the black profiteers who become millionaires through the new minstrelsy and those who would use those new minstrel images to justify the kind of bigotry that our American art, at its very best, lines up against, choosing powerhouse poetry over propaganda. That someone just might be John Singleton.

Segregated Fiction Blues

I. Most Vote for Literary Segregation

From truly ambitious films to thrillers or calculated summer blockbusters, from high-quality television drama to air-headed situation comedies and thirty-second commercial spots, the mass media recognize something in American life that our fiction rarely does. The impression we get from the media is the very same one that just about everybody in the world with access to a television saw during the O.J. Simpson trial. America is now a country with variously positioned ethnic groups whose members function with and against each other, and with and against themselves. If you take a remarkable film like *City of Hope* (1991), written and directed by John Sayles, you get a far from simple picture of a big town. It contains groups on both sides of the color line that have histories, political ambitions, strengths, shortcomings, ambitions, enmities, and so on and on. If you compare the American novel to what Sayles was attempting, one can only say that, in almost all cases, those who chose to express themselves in that form are now are so far behind mass media that one can only be startled.

As Tom Wolfe's "Stalking the Billion-Footed Beast" laid it down fifteen ago, fiction editors at publishing houses gave up expecting to receive books about this roiling, ever more surprising society. Writers chose not to look at where they were and ask themselves if they could decipher the spirit and the contexts of their time. There was plenty of literary theory to back them up. One could be academically up-to-date by deciding to turn away from one's own time. This is just as true now as it was then. Writers have decided that the big sweep of American life out there is something that should be either avoided or broken up into ethnic, religious, sexual, class, and regional franchises. In other words: *If I don't write about you, you won't write about me. I'll stick with my favorite subject—myself—and I suggest you do the same.*

The results have been both dull and dismal. Evasiveness is the order of the day. Over the years Wolfe has been attacked for the kind of literary style he preferred rather than the point he made. He has been dismissed as a "social realist" and in one publication was compared to those in Russia who choked off all creativity with ideological demands. We should not be surprised to see so much horse manure flying from the pitcher's mound because the observations Wolfe made were just a bit too heavy. One could choose to write about this nation in *any* style, from social realist to avant-garde, and still take up Wolfe's challenge. His point is the issue, and it continues to prove itself true. In a time when we see so many people of every color from such a varied range of backgrounds moving across the American scene in the worlds of politics, business, entertainment, science, sports, crime, the military, and just about everything else, American writers of fiction still spend most of their time looking in the opposite direction. They choose to ignore the epic nature of our society as it continues to fight free of its traditional limitations and expectations, or as it tries doctrinaire remedies that are nearly as bad for the body politic as its diseases. While no one has the power or *should* have the right to tell a novelist or a short story writer what he or she has to do, one should not be afraid to say that we do not expect American writers, for the most part, to go beyond themselves. We settle for a crisis born of cowardice, which has determined the convention.

"Cowardice" is the only word that fits because contemporary American writers are hardly lacking in experience or information about other people. This is undeniable. Writers may well have gone to integrated colleges with all manner of people, some of whom have remained their friends over the years. They may live in neighborhoods populated with various kinds of Americans, a few of them friends whose husbands know their husbands, whose wives know their wives, whose kids go to school with their kids, sleep over, party with them, and, as part of a conspiracy to have the very best time possible, go to the same summer camps. These writers may make it their business to associate themselves with at least one version of those organizations bent on chopping down more trees in the poison forest of ethnic, sexual, religious, and class bigotry. Some of their best friends might be—you name it. But when they sit down to write about this big country, they punk out, far, far more often than not.

That is now the norm: punking out. Hiding under the bed. Walking beneath a flag of white underwear stained fully yellow by liquefied fear. Like all forms of cowardice in our moment, there is a self-serving psychological process tailor-made for this particular variation. The lack of aesthetic gumption is remade into a smugness that eventually grants itself a pedigree in narcissism. As life in America becomes an ever more intriguing mix of styles, relationships, alliances, and even combinations of cuisine, things have gotten so mucked up and segregated in the world of literature that one does not expect American writers to tell us about anything other than themselves, their mono-ethnic neighborhoods, their own backgrounds, the narrowest definitions of the classes from which they come, their erotic plumbing and its meaning, how much or how little melanin is in their skin, and so forth.

We do not expect most American fiction to do anything approaching what one sees in the best of dramatic television, which should give any writer a sense of just how much more interesting our human relations have become over the past forty years. At any conventional New York literary party (which is what almost all of them are), if you bring up the subject of something interesting that you saw on television to a writer of American fiction or some supposed expert on the subject, a favorite response is, "Oh, I don't watch television," as if the disclaimer were a badge of intellectual and cultural honor. Given the way it is right now, they would do well to follow that up with, "I don't look at America either." Are we supposed to accept that?

The actual reason we have so little bravery and so little of a special kind of brilliance in contemporary American fiction could easily be the result of the public flogging William Styron took from Negroes for his *Confessions of Nat Turner* (1967), which told the fictionalized story of the slave who led a bloody and squelched revolt in South Carolina in 1831. That Styron was a white Southerner and his subject far removed from his own world (and that of *anyone else* who wasn't alive in the 1830s) was something of a risk, but it wasn't the first such risk taken by a talented white American writer from the South. His most prominent forebear was William Faulkner. In 1940, with *Go*

Down, Moses, Faulkner proved that a white writer from below the Mason-Dixon line (and up to his neck in redneck bile) could do the job to a fare-thee-well. Faulkner not only stepped across the color line a number of times in the book, but he also succeeded in portraying different kinds of Negroes, none of whom fit easily into anybody's stereotypes about poor colored folks down South. He threw down what might be considered the ultimate challenge, a gauntlet with steam rising from it.

Styron was no Faulkner. His book was not good, which may have been one of the reasons that James Baldwin, who was living with the writer and his family while the novel was being created, loved it so and said that it expressed his own feelings with such accuracy that he could have played Styron's Turner in a movie. How now, brown cow? Styron's Nat Turner was an unconvincing Freudian mess of self-hatred, sexual confusion, and panting after just about any white girl's panties—a perfect Baldwin character. That the real Turner was, like John Brown, a brave loon with a good cause that collapsed into bloody slaughter meant that he could have been the inspiration for a first-class and terrifying novel of moral outrage paced by delusions of messianic importance. The circumstances and the context of Turner's brutal revolt were pretty obvious. After all, getting one's throat cut is an occupational hazard of enslaving or terribly oppressing people. Demonic and indifferent treatment from the top can breed demons at the bottom, which the French and Russian revolutions made pretty clear.

A truly important novel might have been written if Styron possessed enough commanding imagination to provide his readers with bracing depictions of the antebellum demons on both ends—the deadly interplay between the institution of slavery and the folk world of superstition and violent visions out of which Turner rose with such confidence in the correctness of his red and sticky work that he pleaded not guilty at his trial. Because, said Prophet Nat, he did not feel he had committed a crime. The hoopla that greeted Styron's book and the scandalously vast praise he received for a job considered very well done would then have been his due. But since the book was not anywhere near a major work, and since its author was arrogant and self-satisfied about it, old Mr. Styron well deserved the brassy spankings he got from so many Negroes intent on turning his bottom cherry red. The intensity of the attacks, however, did not come from an interest in literature but a fairly new conception—that Turner was an ethnic *property*, a black hero who "proved" that there had been slaves who were "real" men, chattels who could put down the plowshare, pick up the sword, and leave fifty-five corpses.

There is an important context here. Styron's book arrived when so-called black revolutionaries had become attractive to a vociferous national body of young black people enthralled by a politics founded in threats of violence, which were known in the streets by the superb slang term "murder-mouthing." Among these saber rattlers the remarkably brave nonviolence of Martin Luther King and his followers was redefined as a form of cowardice, which the slain and canonized Malcolm X had done throughout his brief public career as an attacker of the civil rights movement. So creating a more conventionally masculine main character would have been the "right" thing for Styron to do at the time. Negroes sympathetic to Malcolm X wanted a man who ordered and committed the murders of white men, women, and children. He should have been more Hollywood-derived, more in the tradition of the dime novel heroes of the nineteenth century who found themselves beaming justice and pride while covered with the blood of Indians and desperadoes. This is clearly articulated in *William Styron's*

Nat Turner, Ten Black Writers Respond, edited by John Henrik Clarke. While there is concern about the literary quality of the book, what most offends the gathering is Styron's depiction of Turner as less heroic than what he had come to be in Negro folklore, history, and the political metaphors that amounted to bringing a flame to meet a flame.

In all fairness, the psychological profile that Styron chose to give his Nat Turner could easily have been culled from the speeches of Malcolm X and his autobiography as well as the writing of James Baldwin. Each man spent a good deal of time talking about how much Negroes hated themselves, how cowed they were by whites, how much they wanted to be white; how much, having been taught to look upon them as goddesses, they obsessively lusted after white women. For all of the pilloryings Styron received, he was surely up-to-date with the misreadings of the Negro essence as projected by two of the most famous black men of the 1960s. Even so, the reaction wouldn't have been any different if he had done a superb job, but the book would stand on its own. Spooked, Styron gave up on Negroes and moved on to Jews. *Sophie's Choice* was his next stop. But Styron was not the only one spooked. The impact of the controversy was that white writers at large opted for folding instead of holding, convinced that the challenge of writing across the color line was too big a risk to their careers and their reputations.

They folded for other reasons as well. With the rise of ethnic, female, and sexual preference studies on our college campuses, the idea of being an American writer shrank when it should have expanded. From academe, ethnic groups that once had a very hard time in this country began establishing the argument against *The Confessions of Nat Turner*. They talked of "their" history and "their" people as cultural possessions that shouldn't be tampered with by others for fear of distortion. So-called minorities should be the only ones to handle that material, to assess it, to let everybody know what it means. Whites, forever ready to justify their wrongdoing and praise themselves, couldn't be trusted. All the dirty secrets and lies of the past had to be revealed, heroes recognized, and positive images raised into plain sight. This would lead to social change and liberate those tarred with an imposed vision of innate inferiority.

Since reinterpretation—in the interest of purifying our democracy and moving it beyond its biases—has been basic to the glory of the American tale, there was nothing fundamentally wrong with reexamining what we had been told about each other and what, free of the veils of apology or justification, had actually happened. No, the slaves were not happy to be slaves; every Indian tribe was not a passel of bloodthirsty savages who got what they deserved; Mexicans weren't just a greasy bunch of giggling loafers; Asians weren't subhumanly inscrutable; women had more going for them than their erotic skills, their ability to have babies, and the virtuosity they brought to housekeeping. These were important insights to make common knowledge and so were the many achievements and contributions made by Americans of every hue, religion, and both sexes to the development of this nation.

Had that been what we actually got, from hoot to snoot, things might be very different in American fiction. In the past forty years, we have come a long way from the era when there were no black mayors of major cities, when we didn't think about women in politics or business, when our films and our television shows would give the once proverbial Martian the impression that those who were not white were either servants or victims of society or existed almost solely for cheap thrills or comic relief. But that once proverbial Martian would get a much stronger sense of what the United States is about these days if he or she or it were to spend a week or two looking at HBO or Showtime around the clock instead of reading American fiction. The idea of exclusive cultural property has so taken hold that writers are not encouraged to find themselves material that will ask them to move under the skins of people unlike themselves. Writers are encouraged to never leave home.

I have been told by some who have endured them, that in one writing workshop after another the territorial limits are so confining that anyone who steps outside of what he or she happens to be in terms of class or sex or ethnicity or sexual persuasion receives a scolding from both instructors and other writers. Yet these workshops are not opposed to encouraging the pompous side of emblematic cultural possession, which amounts to exotica that falls far short of the metaphor for life at large that the most talented bring to the tight focus on a community or a special group or a class, as Susan Minot so wonderfully illustrated in *Evening*. In essence, Hemingway's dictum of writing about what you know has become an excuse for avoiding risks. Since Hemingway wrote about a wide mix of people, some American, some not, it's clear the great writer wasn't advising those who took up his craft to isolate themselves from the world. When Hemingway said that not knowing the language of a foreign country was bad for a writer because it denied him the eavesdropping that provided so many insights, he was obviously giving another dimension to writing about what you know. What you know might be something you took the time and went somewhere to discover.

This has not been missed by everyone. When Tom Wolfe spoke to the Washington Press Club a few years ago, he wondered why more writers didn't pick up the challenge laid down by Richard Price in *Clockers*. As Wolfe observed, Price got up

off his rusty dusty and left his home in Manhattan to explore
the crack world in a New Jersey housing project. Price learned
how it worked and wrote a convincing novel filled with characters who were vastly different from himself. Cormac McCarthy
did an equally ambitious job with his little-known play, *The Stone
Mason*. It is about three generations of Negroes trying to hold
themselves together even as their chances and their cohesion
are drained by the values of the streets and the mistakes of
those who don't know how to manage a business. In addition
to the environment, both Price and McCarthy captured the
humanity of the voices, which is the essence of the dialogue
that elevates such material above pretension and superficiality.
Price and McCarthy provide something that wouldn't have surprised writers of the nineteenth century, who loved to roll up
their sleeves and arm-wrestle with the demands of capturing
the masses and the asses and the classes.

I do not mean sociology, which is what those miffed by the
idea that they should know anything about this nation always
retreat into defending themselves against. I mean something on
the level of what this nation is, this country so steeped in tragic
optimism. We Americans are fascinated by the relationship of
the individual to the mass. We are both wary of and attracted to
the stranger. We like to be by ourselves but we feel completed
when we're inside the right kind of crowd. Because we came
into existence as a nation by rebelling against Great Britain, our
love of the rebel is understandable but unfortunately naive
(as with the ongoing "rage against the establishment" that has
become the conventional ethos of the multibillion dollar industry of rap and rock and roll). Our social contract is built on the
principle of making sure that power is not abused, and we have
great suspicion of government. But because we have known
truly great leaders, such as Lincoln, there is also a nostalgia for

someone who will bring us together or lead us through the storm we feel we have been in too long. In our own American way, we are as open to a Martin Luther King Jr. as we are to the false prophets and impostors Borges parades through his *Universal History of Infamy.* Elijah Muhammad, Jim Jones, Jim Bakker, and David Koresh provide easy examples.

The historical and political parts of our collective identity give us a range of dispositions and appetites for human tales. Since ours is a society that sees the idea of upward mobility proven over and over in the worlds of startling new fortunes, we love stories that detail the trouble of moving from the bottom up to the top just as much as we gobble up stories about the trouble and the heartbreak in the mansions on the peaks. The very nature of our culture and history, from the collision between Europeans and Indians to the struggles involving class, religion, sex, and region, inclines us to appreciate tales that pivot on the difficulties of recognizing the humanity of people who come from social situations quite unlike ours. The freedom or lack of freedom to reinvent oneself is another favorite, as is the story of a person who is so well acquainted with the range of stuff out there that he or she seems almost a chameleon. Hawthorne's paranoid world has grown to include scandals in law enforcement, government, and the sharkier waters of business. (Hawthorne would not, perhaps *could not*, have ignored the meaning of the murderous destruction of the house in Waco, a harrowing example of hysteria folded coldly into military maneuvers, its intended outcome made clear by the footage of those men firing on anyone trying to escape the flames by one of the doors. When we take the face of David Koresh and line it up with the schoolmarm mug of Janet Reno, we see that both the handsome and the homely can abuse religious faith or defend indefensible actions in a nation where people are not supposed

to be murdered for being crazy and dangerous. Those are serious
literary subjects.) We stay attuned to the ongoing battles we must
fight to keep society on a democratic course and are captivated
by tales that address the many obstacles of corruption, superstition, ignorance, contempt, and opportunism. There is, at the
center of this nation's soul, a tragic optimism that recognizes our
capacity for folly, corruption, mediocrity, and incompetence but
maintains belief in the possibility of meeting those eternal
human failings with enough force to whack them down until
they make their inevitable return.

If more of our writers, in whatever styles they choose and
from whatever perspectives they wish, address these epic complexities and appetites, our literature will become richer and so
will our nation and so will the American story that is so intriguing to the entire globe.

II. Others Don't

One thing you can always be sure about in America is that no
matter how strong a convention is, no matter how well rational-
ized, some will say hooey through their efforts to get something
else done. That is why, even for all of the obstacles described
above, there is a literary movement afoot that has not yet been
noticed by our establishment. It is, in fact, the most significant
movement in American fiction, the one that recognizes the
frontier where all of the issues of integration are raised. If we
examine the perennial themes of boy meets girl, God and man,
goods and services, nature and man, the forces driving to maintain or dismantle the policies that hold a certain political order
in place, and just about anything else, we discover that integration may be the most important theme in literature. That is all
writers have ever talked about: how two things quite different or

seemingly different can be brought together. As the talk gets deep enough to achieve what we call the literary, the inevitable demons of folly, corruption, incompetence, and mediocrity—which arrive within every form of society—show their power and test people about whom we are told a story.

Within the context of our society, the "I and thou" issue begets a complex set of questions. Most American writers rarely take up the challenges Faulkner laid down when he tried to make sense of what has happened to us—white, black, Indian, Asian, animal, and nature. He examined where we meet and where we part and why. He knew that apprehending the other in terms of mutual humanity is the task and the trouble. To the good, there are contemporary writers who do not accept the handwriting on the wall because they want to know what is on the other side of it. They are digging under it, boring holes in it, and, if those don't work, they are climbing over it.

In two Philip Roth novels, *American Pastoral* (1997) and *The Human Stain* (2000), we get examples of the problems of imagination in our fiction as well as a marvelous rejoinder. First, the problem. In *American Pastoral*, a flawed masterpiece, we see a quite revealing example of the trouble our fiction has in moving across ethnic lines based on color. This novel is grounded in meditation and endless questioning. The central character is a Jewish guy named Seymour Lebov but nicknamed "the Swede" for his handsome Nordic looks and athletic physique. He's doing all right with his Irish American wife and their child until everything goes wacky. Completely. The Swede mulls for five years over his life and his family and the world around them, seeking an understanding, a source, a tradition, a trend out of which his daughter's actions came to violent flower. She has disappeared into the hot underground of late 1960s radical politics after becoming a mad bomber for the cause of rattling America and opposing the war in Vietnam. Her commitment to "bring-ing the war home" results in the unintentional homicide of a harmless old bystander she blows up in the local post office. Collateral damage.

During one of the moonless nights of his soul, Angela Davis, the brown madonna of the revolution, appears to the Swede in the kitchen of his home in Eastern Seaboard Anglo country, where the estates are big and the family lines long. Here is the great flaw in the book. For all of this man's deeply specu-lative meditations, he never wonders—even once—how Angela Davis became what she was and how her actions must have struck her middle-class family from Birmingham, Alabama. She couldn't have been born that way. What steps led to her trans-formation? Were her parents as shocked as the Swede and his wife? Was their sense of the world as shaken? If they didn't have the same general emotional reactions, why not? Were they red diaper Negroes so committed to leftist revolution that nothing else mattered? If not, how might they have felt when their bril-liant daughter, who had studied at the Sorbonne, became a fist-waving cheerleader for the violent overthrow of the United States? If he contacted them, could they be of any help in crack-ing the underground where the Swede's daughter was hiding? Might the Swede better understand his daughter's transforma-tion if he understood Angela Davis's? What could have been in Davis's mind when she wrote love letters to an imprisoned black felon who fancied himself a revolutionary ready to kill for black liberation? Was she guilty or not when Davis found herself on the run for purported involvement in a botched jailbreak in San Rafael, California, one so filled with blunders that it resulted in a number of deaths?

Hold it. A writer as gifted as Roth is obviously not required to do anything other than what he chooses, but his failure of imagination reduces the reality of the era into which he was looking. Contrary to the impression the book gives, the situation with this kind of girl is not something that only happened to white folks. Parents across the color spectrum were startled, horrified, and sometimes thrust into tragedies because their children went off the deep end of anarchic politics. This tragedy in the ranks of the most radical was very different from the collective one that was intensified by the southern racists who murdered the non-violent black and white civil rights workers protesting the conventions of segregation and the exclusion of Negroes from the political process. Their bravery and their sacrifice pulled the mask off of southern hospitality and exposed the dark, ruthless power of an order held in place by terrorism.

The new superradicals arrived in the wake of the black power movement, which declared itself in 1966. Many came from blue-collar or middle-class families that expected them to forge successful careers. Those black parents were as bewildered as Roth's central character when their children, swept up in the politics of the time, turned against a flawed society and sought to destroy it, spurning every promise and every example of gradual social change. Consequently and unfortunately, Roth's tight focus on the troubles of one family comprising two white ethnic groups segregates the tale from the actual body heat of its time. It reduces the complexity of what his major character would come to understand about the national dimensions of his sorrow and how it transcended segregated ideas about color and class. If he spent five years thinking and didn't come to recognize something about that, the Swede is the dumbest character Roth ever invented.

Roth, always a master for all that, proves that he could have done a better job of bringing more worlds to the page. He superbly summons the three-dimensional, flesh-and-blood

presence of the Miss America Pageant of 1948, the inner life
and working-class background of the protagonist's Irish wife,
and the condescending Yankees who make it clear to this Jew
that he is a late arrival in the long tale of America. This is
unmentioned but intentionally proven by a tour in which the
Swede is shown all of the Yankee family plots in the town
graveyard. They reach back a few centuries. Unlike the Swede,
not one of them is a peasant who made a bundle running a
glove factory in the cultural outhouse of Newark, New Jersey.

That this story is not told by the main character but is imagined by Nathan Zuckerman, who went to high school with him,
doesn't let Roth off the hook. We learn from earlier novels that
imagining wild lives for others—or impersonating his own imag-
inings—is a speciality of Zuckerman's. Though many critics
complained that Zuckerman made a strong appearance for seventy pages or so then disappeared, they were wrong. He never
disappears. The whole book is his. Roth gives us a number of
clues based in the fictional writer's crude and shocking sexual
obsessions. We become absolutely sure that the writer of *American Pastoral* is Zuckerman when the Swede looks under Angela
Davis's dress as her apparition materializes in his kitchen. That
is Zuckerman's style, not the Swede's, and Roth the genius trick-
ster knows it. Had Roth let Zuckerman go after Davis's consciousness and background, the writer might have brought the
whole thing off even more forcefully. Wasn't there someone,
aware of the continuity it would have given to Roth's other work,
who could have suggested such possibilities to him? Why
wouldn't Roth's editor have suggested something to him that
would have taken Roth far outside of the conventions of contemporary fiction? A good question. Did his editor fear Roth's
reaction? More probably the reason is simply an unimaginative
sense of American life. I would bet on that. Almost never fails.

The Human Stain helps move forward the epic possibilities of contemporary American fiction. It has its flaws, as do all books that take on the formal and conceptual challenges Roth brings to the table. The freedom of narrative line that he has invented for himself is put to fresh uses as he details the surfaces and explores the subsurfaces of his characters. Here he engages the theme of "passing," the term that Negroes use for those who have skin light enough to cross into the territory of white folks and experience the freedoms that color would have blocked from them. By taking on this theme, Roth is able to look into status strategies as American as those Fitzgerald revealed in *The Great Gatsby*, which Albert Murray has described in conversation as "the most famous novel about passing ever written." The ethnic particulars slide right into the remaking of the self that is so basic to our social history, due to the density of our population and the breadth of our continent.

By crossing color and class lines, by appropriating and making use of protean figures from Greek and Roman mythology, by sending up the ongoing French invasion of our academies through the hilarious and monstrously devious character of Delphine Roux, by paralleling the buffoonish sexual acts that Monica Lewinsky performed on Bill Clinton with tragedies inside the novel, and by spinning out his own variations on Hemingway's love of the outdoors and his portraits of men emotionally mangled by war, Roth has taken a leading position among those rising up against the segregated nature of contemporary fiction. He remains himself, with his ever unique quality of light, but helps point to a fresh path for our imaginative narrative writing.

In *The Human Stain*, Roth gives us the kind of omnidirectional sense of the skinny that would have made *American Pastoral* nearly perfect had he used it there. This time out, he shoots for an overview of America that lines up the parallels and the contrasts that create a national experience. His central contention is that American life, regardless of color or religion or money, always finds itself at odds with the wildness at the center of the national soul, the anarchic impulses that only achieve vitality when there is enough grace, however hard-won, to get past our penchant for destruction. Achieving that grace takes time and a willingness to endure the punches that others feel it their duty to lay on, whether firmly in the face or even more firmly in the back. The real preference could be wielding the gutting knife while the victim is tied to a table. After such an experience, one surely needs time to get it together.

Time is something Americans never have enough of, which sometimes results in quick fixes that are grounded in childishness. This inevitably leads to the creation of one puritanical order after another, each one heatedly looking for the villain who can be blamed for all the difficulty. Perhaps the villain is the economic system, maybe the government, could be the Jew or the Negro or the Asian, perhaps sex, perhaps the bigot, there is always the politically incorrect way of teaching, and let us not forget that the Great Satan could be the institutions that put into policy whatever our latest ideas about ourselves are. In the angry soap opera that is a response to the depths, darknesses, and disillusionments of American existence, a happy ending is sought—demanded—no matter how much blood must be poured into each chair so that the viewer will be stuck in place.

That is why *The Human Stain*, like almost all serious American fiction bent on understanding the darker nature of the country—raw dog without a bag—must look the violent right in the face. This novel is rooted in Hawthorne, Melville, Twain, Fitzgerald, Hemingway, Faulkner, and Ellison. There is literal violence aplenty—wife beating, war, boxing, street brawls, and murder. There is also the sanctimonious violence of pushing the scarlet letter of accusation onto someone who simply does not adhere to the thoughtless processes through which we clumsily attempt to address our nation's diversity. The assumption is that no member of a group that has historically been the victim of bigotry should be expected to stand up to pressure or recognize the layering of meaning central to sophisticated human intercourse. Too much for them.

The main character is Coleman Silk, who has spent years passing for white in the humanities department he developed for a small liberal arts college called Athena. After nearly forty years as a professor of classics and the dean of faculty, Silk shovels some damning stuff at the fan when he asks his class about registered students who have not shown up six weeks into the semester. "Does anyone know these people? Do they exist or are they spooks?" The term "spooks" is interpreted as a racial slur and Silk is brought up on charges of racism because the students he has never seen are black. Silk cannot dismiss the charge by calling up his own ethnic identity because he has hidden it for many years. From there, everything goes downhill.

Hawthorne seems to become progressively more important to Roth. He is concerned with the vulgar appetite for betrayal that seems to reside in the very molecules of American air. Roth grasps well the mass hysteria that derails the idea of democratic rule and the imposition of scarlet letters, which remake people and their reputations until both stand in for chamber pots. In *The Human Stain* he shows us that today's scarlet letters are, depending on the position in the field, labels like "liberal," "conservative," "Uncle Tom," "sexist," and "racist." In the hands of ideologues and opportunists such terms (emptied of their legitimate meanings) are used to intimidate or to silence. Those scarlet letters wield the most power on college campuses, where freedom of speech and thought are scarcely allowed. Silk, seemingly out of nowhere, experiences the droll totalitarianism that frightens contemporary college academics into shape. No one stands behind him or speaks up for him. The word "spook" was too much. His peers know how things have changed. One must keep up. One must watch what one says, not step on anyone's toes, and be especially sure to respect the feelings of those from among the downtrodden—who may be hypersensitive, but what is one to expect, given their history in this society? The most important rule is to be ready to pull down and pile onto any who do not recognize the importance of going along with the program.

"People in Athena know perfectly well that this is not the case," writes Roth, "and yet, as in the spooks incident, they willingly act as if they don't. Simply to make the accusation is to prove it. To hear the allegation is to believe it. No motive for the perpetrator is necessary, no logic or rationale is required. Only a label is required. The label is the motive. The label is the evidence. The label is the logic."

Silk is embittered by his colleagues' cowardice, their fashionableness, and the bureaucratic cruelty that is especially difficult for an intellectual man of action, a former athlete, to handle—though he was never been bad at it himself. The pressure on him and the charges of racism have damaged his sanity, but despite hard shocks such as his wife's sudden death from heart failure, Silk is able to maintain an invented story of his life. He delivers it with an odd combination of rage and aplomb to Nathan Zuckerman, who is back on the case. Zuckerman is in New England to write but seems drafted by fate to delve into who Silk was after he dies, with a young woman, in an automobile accident, falling in brutal violence like some hopelessly doomed character from Greek mythology.

The trouble in the academy, the wages of Vietnam, the anger inspired by love, and the dirty facts of passing from one world into the next are the novel's themes. All provide Roth with his orchestration of sensibility, class, race, and sex into a symphonic investigation of loss, of the immutable and indelible blues of being alive. Nothing can ever be recaptured or made right. Once it has happened and the change has come, one cannot return to what one was or see the world as one once did. Roth is saying to us that all sensitive people, their origins be damned, are scheduled to lose their illusions. There is no such thing as revenge because, as the Greeks repeatedly learned to no avail, force is never more than futile; it leaves its mark wherever it falls but does not change the thing that has been brought down by an earlier slight or a previous injustice. All wounds are permanent.

If lucky, the lion in winter, with snow up to his chin, will encounter a young lioness who believes that her greatest power is the willingness to do anything in private, to seize joy, to provide comfort, to discover, even against her will, that the slim chance at love has fattened up and appeared in a lover twice her age. The young lioness is Faunia, whose children were killed in a fire upstairs while she was performing a "Lewinsky" downstairs. Upstairs Blues Downstairs, or Downstairs Blues Upstairs. Faunia's husband is a raging Vietnam vet who boils over at the memory of his ex-wife's infidelity and the heartbreaking results of it. He has, for all practical purposes, lost his senses under twin blows—war memories and the actions of his wife, who feels no less scraped empty by the victims of her negligence.

These three people have the disruption of their worlds in common and Zuckerman, his pipe and deerstalker's hat in place, does his expected detective work. He imagines the meaning of it all as he has been doing since *The Ghost Writer*, beginning with the facts and embroidering them with his understanding of the jungle we call the human interior. Throughout the novel, the world of Greek myth resonates and the vision we discover in this novel is another sort of Oedipus, a man eventually destroyed by trying to avoid his fate—fleeing his home to avoid the prophecy of killing his father and marrying his mother. Oedipus, always an arrogant son of a bitch, unknowingly kills his actual father on the public road and ends up in bed with his mother, unaware and self-satisfied. Silk fled what Baldwin called the "doom of color" only to be brought down by a couple of Negro kids who have been granted the ability to destroy through accusation.

Roth's imagination is so fine-tuned that he reinterprets classical aspects of the passing novel without, he says, ever having read one. Silk's father, mother, sister, and brother are well etched, startlingly so for anyone who is not aware of what a real writer can do. The fact that Coleman chooses to trade in his actual identity for that of a Jew—on the advice of a Jew—is a savvy perception of the moment in the late 1940s when it was less social bad fortune to be a Jew than a Negro in America— George Gershwin, Hank Greenberg, Bess Myerson and all of that. (Some might point out that since Leo Frank is the only Jew ever strung up in the public purging of imagined demons known as lynching, it was less bad fortune from the moment significant numbers of Jews began arriving in the United States in the 1890s.)

Those who have some sense of how Roth thinks were not surprised that he would be inspired by the story of Anatole Broyard because Broyard—uh-oh—had slighted the depth of Roth's knowledge of women in *Kafka Was the Rage*. The book was a posthumous memoir as remarkable for its portraits of Manhattan during the late 1940s, 1950s, and the early 1960s as it was for how tightly Broyard, a New Orleans Creole, kept his white mask in place. Broyard had made his bed and Roth chose to make him lie in it when he called the Jewish writer out by saying, "In *Portnoy's Complaint*, Portnoy says that underneath their skirts girls all have cunts. What he didn't say—this was his real trouble, his real complaint—was that underneath their skirts they also had souls. When they were undressed, I saw their souls as well as their cunts. They wore their souls like negligees that they never took off. And one man in a million knows how to make love to a soul."

Those were fighting words; and the wonder of Philip Roth is that he decided, somewhere along the way, to make Coleman Silk as human as he could and prove that he could see the soul of Faunia clothing her skin as well as the intangible but palpable human quality in the other women he depicts. Roth parodies the monstrous Delphine Roux by having her symbolically born in a torrent of urine. This sweet-smelling soul of vanguard academic convention falls for Coleman Silk but, in an allusion to Kundera's *The Letter*, pushes in the mad accusation of misogyny while he is down on one knee and cannot defend himself.

That is what makes *The Human Stain* so interesting. Roth rises to challenges (or sets challenges for himself) that take him beyond the territory that his genius usually explores. He has made the most of the parallels between Zuckerman and Silk. Zuckerman was often at odds with the vision of Jewish identity and responsible behavior that surrounded him as a young man in Newark, and Silk is at odds with accepting the limitations of color that he can easily duck because so little melanin makes its presence known in his face. Unlike almost all Negroes, Silk can choose, and choose he does, which results in his being barred from his own family by his brother, who sees him as "a traitor to his race" and a coward, though his sister keeps in touch with him. Though Coleman Silk had a loving wife and four children, there was only one person, as Bessie Smith said, who "knew his name."

As with *American Pastoral*, the emotions inspired by his theme of loss seem melancholic extensions of Roth's earlier work, though he maintains an intentionally crude sexual candor that prevents those on the right from embracing his attacks on political correctness, which in turn forces those on the left to grind their teeth at his every word about the new totalitarianism. The puritanical right cannot forgive him his erotic explicitness, and the left will never get past his portrayal of the cowardice and the equally puritanical joy at bringing superior people down that has always been the greatest flaw in left-wing orthodoxy. No. Philip Roth will not be held into a simply defined position, and that is why his example has a particular importance to the motion on the contemporary frontier of American fiction.

Danzy Senna was twenty-eight when her first novel, *Caucasia*, was published in 1998. She is one of the leaders of the pack and could be, given the amount that she already understands and is able to bring to the page, either a genius or somebody in a photo finish with the definition. I say that because there is a more than special level of perception and feeling in her novel, which is about one of a pair of girls born to a black man and a white woman. Despite the imbecilic and simpleminded things said about race and class today—just like yesterday!—a serious writer is expected to be intelligent about the matter and snap free to some kind of special brightness, if possessed of enough talent. But Senna's gift is that her emotions meet her intelligence and they go toe to toe, neither winning out over the other. I don't know if that's correct, but she is able to bring so much feeling to her tale, while remaining sardonic, pitiless, whimsical, and empathetic. Sure, we expect anger and violence in contemporary American art that takes on the worlds of color, but we don't expect so many moments of pathos, tenderness, love—unrequited or not—as Senna delivers with a sailing power that rises above mush. Senna's heroine is notable for being conceived with striking originality and for the swirls of pointed intellect and nuanced emotion that animate her.

The girl, whose name is Birdy, can pass for white or something close to it, unlike her sister, whose ethnicity is clear a mile away. Her father is an academic who believes that there is a kind of freedom for black people in Brazil that does not exist in America. When he and his wife break up, the father takes Colette, the dark-skinned girl, with him, leaving the white mother and her dangerously light-skinned daughter behind. The mother, a fat, upper-class Bostonian, has to take Birdy on the run after she gets mixed up in some "revolutionary" stuff with a gaggle of charismatic and delusional Negroes. As the mother loses her identity and has to keep inventing another for herself and her daughter, Senna moves us through a number of cultural variations that are precisely drawn and just as precisely felt.

Birdy, who had always felt an outsider among Negroes benumbed by black nationalism, eventually becomes, for all practical purposes, white and watches her mother trim down from stress until a slim, attractive woman appears. Her mother is far different, in certain ways, than she was when men had to be captivated by her mind in order to accept her voluminous body. But Birdy is not comfortable being a white girl or some sort of exotic. She feels no bitterness toward white people for being white or for being different from Negroes. She takes them on one at a time and makes her decisions about them on the basis of how they come off to her as individuals. In that sense, she is different from both her father and her mother; her pops ties the world down with theories, while her moms, as soon as she feels free in their little home on the run, shows her new, small ass with the kind of contempt for convention and sense of superiority common to upper-class white radicals. But because Senna is such an artist, one observes this and puts it together without ever being literally told any such thing. As the two settle in New Hampshire, the narrative calms down and Birdy's observations and recollections are those of a young woman growing up and seeing the world ever more clearly. Her body is on the ground but her mind stays on vacation.

Birdy's dream is to reunite with her sister somehow, someday, somewhere. As a wanderer, she realizes that she does not have a geographical home. Cole, the nickname for Birdy's sister, is her home, not her father, not her mother. Or at least she thinks her real home is her sister. Mottled emotionally in so many ways by the nature of humanity, Birdy believes that her relationship to her sister had always been pure. It sailed up above her father's race theories, above the hostility that her father's new black wife had toward her, above her mother's radical politics, anger, and self-pity. As Senna shows us, there is a bond between the two girls that is much more real than any of the conventions of identity that mashed down on them through the voodoo politics and costumed ethnicity of the 1970s, when they were growing up. It remains more true in Birdy's memory than the settling into paranoia, rhetorical disdain, and bitterness that characterized the lives of most radicals who made it to the 1980s. Once it became clear that "the revolution" was never coming, radicals discovered the harsh facts of failed and foolish ideas. All that was left for the bulk of them was the dull prison of academic life, the resentment expressed in voting as far left as possible, and the embittering new identities that the most extreme had to create in order to remain outside of the prison system.

That, of course, is easy to say; it is hard to write, and that is why Senna is so notable. She makes us feel the humanity of her people, no matter where on the color spectrum or the class ladder they exist. Her sympathy to all people and her contempt for fools and her understanding of folly form a powerful perspective that is run through with humor of the witty or gut-busting or gallows kind. Senna also understands how new orders are not necessarily new and that their power relationships are usually based on assumptions that are usually no more than alternate versions of an aristocracy, an elect, a group of special people. Intellectuals, revolutionaries, lower-, middle-, and upperclass people have a strong sense of what makes someone special, more important to listen to, better to be around, a more perfect model to imagine for themselves.

Senna's Birdy fits into none of those categories. She is emotionally free in no world other than the one she and her sister invented for themselves, which had its own language and was untranslatable by outsiders. When she was young, the revved up black students at the black nationalist school rejected Birdy for being too white looking and she felt guilty for not having hair that was woolly, like her sister's. She is sure that that is why her father chose to leave with her sister and not her. Her mother is left with a child who should be easier to rear because Birdy's grandmother is more comfortable with her than with her sister, and, perhaps, so is her mother. In her adventures on the run with her mother and her observations about the nature of life as she meets it, Birdy functions impeccably as a flesh-and-blood woman through which Senna shows us how much she knows about America and how well a writer can bring to life the variety of this nation in its grandeur, its petty delusions, its infinite speech patterns, its mystery, its race and class tensions.

When Birdy and her mother go on the run and reinvent themselves as a widowed mother and half-Jewish daughter, they have actually realized a tendency common to their time of ethnic and "street" masking. Birdy's deeply intellectual father and other black people slide in and out of forced street slang, slogans, and street bits of performance that they believe give them greater authenticity and proves their obliviousness, even if only recently discovered, to "white" grammar and deportment. This was part of the mythology that developed as a supposed freedom from "white culture." Whites might seek a freedom from "bourgeois privilege," which meant embracing Negro art and politics, Eastern religions, and folk dress from the world over. But the pressure on them was nowhere near as strong. There was no white "authenticity" against which they were measured. Senna exposes the doctrinaire ways in which black children can be forced into assuming postures that are intellectual constructs imposed on behavior, the inventions of politicians, sociologists, and psychologists. Children then seek to be good automatons, not individuals, and feel terrible when they don't do well at erasing their human qualities. The horror of it all is that the response to stereotyping was an ingroup stereotyping with the intended results of group loyalty spelled out in specific behavior and specific lingo.

What makes *Caucasia* such a particular event is that it is not a rant, but a complicated human picture of a number of worlds that we have not seen so well investigated before, or brought together with such clarity. The lucidity of this epic rendering allows us to recognize those varied worlds as part of the ongoing American dilemma of identity, which is deepened in its complexity as more and more cultures from outside of the West become available. They are borrowed from or pillaged into the superficial condition of kitsch or drawn on as actual inspiration or rejected if they prove that in their quaint and exotic qualities they are, finally, inadequate tools for facing modern circumstances. Danzy Senna is a gifted young contender who could easily emerge in her maturity as a champion of our literature.

Joyce Carol Oates is a seasoned champ, and, in terms of the subject of this chapter, only a lightweight would be surprised to find her assuming a high position in the effort. As with the lamenting interracial romance of *Because It Is Bitter, And Because It Is My Heart* (1990), Oates is at it again. *I'll Take You There* (2003) is a much better book about class prejudice, interracial love, and the mucky situation of a girl rejected by her father. As expected, she is after the same thing seen in Roth from a wholly different perspective. Oates seeks out the human meanings of our troubles and our victories and proposes by example that a writer of fiction can step up and write, denying innate barriers to human feeling and human revelation: one does not have to be "one of them" in order to "understand" those other people. No one has chosen to go further or deeper than Oates in this regard. Few can actually say what her ambitions are because she has written so many books. One would have to be very, very dedicated to find out all that is actually on her mind. One thing is sure: she will climb as many walls as necessary to present us with something of human value as she understands the term.

I'll Take You There is an avant-garde novel in its structure of three movements that function like long musical choruses in which themes are laid out, symbols are manipulated, and the very tools that will appear at the end, like the mirror, keep expanding on themselves as the narrator, a woman writer, recalls three events from her early womanhood that she realizes are related because they all brought her closer to maturity. In each case she moves from macro to micro, from some big theme or some big situation to something very intimate, a moment between the narrator and one other person. She moves from a class situation in a sorority house to an interracial romance to a confrontation with the face of death as it appears in a mirror used to secretly look at a dying parent.

Each of the movements is about a spirit enduring rejection and surmounting its own sorrow and its own fear, sometimes asserting itself through a defensive anger that can be self-deprecating or mockingly aggressive. The novel is about six things: self-confidence, bigotry, class, race, parentage, and geography. A naive, insecure, brilliant girl discovers that her sorority sisters are no more than crude, well-reared cows possessed of little other than self-love, sadism, and prejudices. The British house mistress whom she admires is as lonely as the narrator and drinks in private, more than anyone should know. The girl leaves the sorority, pretending to be part Jewish—which is worse than already being poor—and the house mistress is brought down by the girl's curiosity.

This theme of leaving and destruction is carried out when the same young, slim girl later falls for a willfully hazy Negro student of philosophy ten years her senior. Profoundly self-obsessed, he pretends not to want her anymore than the snooty sorority sisters did. Feeling a camaraderie because she too is an outsider, the girl believes that her experience with the class prejudices of the sorority have given her the power to love him against all odds and cure him of his vast loneliness, even find herself in the process. She is wrong and he dogs her, which she accepts as a young woman of her sort would. Bored and intimidated by her ardent—even sacrificial—willingness, he furiously drops the girl when he catches her rummaging through his stuff, just as she did the private possessions of the sorority house mistress, who also caught her. Yet she has come to know him in the same way that she came to know the house mistress, by using a detective's logic as she studies his private papers and his secreted photographs. Again, she realizes how a person feels and what this person has done in that mystery we call the past.

We see those things based in color prejudice that separate the girl and her lover, the botherment of being on display and always poorly understood when they are sometimes doing their best to understand each other, to rise above the loneliness they have in common so that they can offer each other something truly personal, neither emblematic nor desperate. Some of these things arrive in sexual revelations that are as deep as anything James Joyce has told us and far deeper than what most American writers have had to say, even when sex sustains itself as an obsession. The way the young woman stands up to the corpulent dean of students who is disturbed by her sleeping with a Negro shows both the girl's courage and, in a masterful turn, her gloating pride at not being a bigot or a coward. This gives us the human feeling of a certain kind of youngish liberalism in all its brashness and naive sense of signal accomplishment.

The interracial romance is delivered with subtle insights that address color while stepping above it. Her guy does not see himself in terms of his skin tone because he believes that he has "a higher calling," which is to say that he wants to put his mind in dialogue with the great philosophers, as a man, not a person completely defined by color. She, being more than a bit astute, realizes at one point that all of the philosophers are men and they must have had penises—just as her guy must reluctantly realize that he does. But, the narrating older woman realizes, the presence and the appetites of a penis are never the subjects of philosophy. That her guy is an intellectual means that she loves him because they can talk about philosophy and hide their needs behind ideas. This is very touching since it is the way young people are who discover that they, unlike most who surround them, are given to thoughts and questions. They can excitedly hide behind their minds the way others hide behind rituals or fashion or social position or their own faces and figures. The talk is no less jive; it is just of a higher and more charming order.

The achievement of the work, other than the masterful strength of the form, the improvisational attitude toward sentence structure, and the foreshadowing as well as the deft use of motifs, is that the world is revealed through a totally self-obsessed person whose entire experience is lived while closely contemplated under the microscope of her own mind. The challenge is to get other characters through the screen of her self-consciousness, which Oates does as only a true commander of the telling detail can. In the process, she proves to us why this character is a fiction writer, as no one other than a writer could be so attentive, both to herself and to those who are important to her, whether in good or bad ways.

While using the overriding issues of philosophy—meaning, presence, nuance, explanation—the novelist brings to life the sorority bitches and reveals something only the most insightful novelists realize, which is that alienation, *like* worshipful acceptance, creates a vulgar narcissism. The overwhelmed outsider suffers from constant self-perusal, wondering whether one is accepted or not, is worthy of acceptance or should be rejected, looks right or does not, is truly inferior or, Lord help us, superior. But in the world of white folks, it can go ever further than that. Skin might not be enough. When the girl pretends to be Jewish in order to challenge the prejudices of the sorority, Oates shows us how merely claiming an ethnicity can change how one is seen, or not seen. Prior to that, she was only thought of as a bumbling girl from some farm town in upstate New York. Now she has added ethnic prejudice to the class prejudice she is already experiencing. In short, she has become more repulsive, a condition she pushes even further by picking a Negro lover.

By the final movement, it all comes down to a little house in which the girl's father is dying and the house mistress is a woman with whom he has lived and either has married or has not. The girl drove from Vermont, where she is finishing her first book, all the way out west to Utah. Here, in the big spaces of the West, so much is about sight, about confronting the impersonality of nature, about thinking something is one thing from a distance and coming close enough to realize that it is something else altogether. It is also about how small our lives are in the world of nature; unlike the grand narcissism of philosophy, nature needs never to know, or care, about the meaning of anything. People appear and disappear. They are remembered and they are not. But if they are remembered accurately enough, they remain part of the public record until the public and the record have disappeared at the behest of the butcher known as time.

In the song that may have inspired the title of this novel, the Staple Singers tell us that they know of a place where nobody is crying, where no one is worried, where there are no false smiling faces, where there is no lying to the races, and that they can take us there. Joyce Carol Oates is telling us exactly the opposite but, instead of depressing us, she lifts our spirits with the tragic optimism that is at the center of her poetic impulse, a force that, word by word, never fails to rise up from the dark, sorrowing innards of this novel.

These three examples are connected by ambition, force, and freshness to a growing body of work. Some of the most ambitious are Ralph Ellison's *Juneteenth*, Edward P. Jones's *The Known World*, Richard Powers's *The Time of Our Singing*, Robert Hellenga's *Blues Lesson*, Barbara Probst Solomon's *Smart Hearts for the City*, Andrea Lee's *Interesting Women*, Charles Johnson's *Ox-Herding Tale* (and the novels that have followed), Lore Segal's *My First American* (which might be a masterpiece), Bharati Mukerjee's *The Middleman and Other Stories*, Tom Piazza's *Blues and Trouble*, Richard Price's recent novels, and, of course, the fiction of Tom Wolfe. Whether one likes those books or not, whether they succeed or fail or partially achieve their intentions, is less important than their shared stance. Writers such as these have chosen to test themselves by finding out if they have the imagination to render vividly and believably people unlike the ones they grew up next door to, which is, as I have repeatedly said, a quite uncommon activity in these dark and dull days of pervasive literary cowardice.

Blues Plate Special

OVER THE TELEPHONE, FROM SOMEWHERE IN NEW England, the maestro speaks.

Everybody is on a very strange course. No one has the capacity to think the whole thing through. Given my capacities, when I was a young man I behaved as though I was going to get to the bottom of it, but I don't know that any of us are capable of making much headway. After all is said and all is done, we are stuck in the middle of something we are forever trying to understand. In every period, we must recognize, understanding is a problem unique to the circumstances that present themselves— whether anybody likes those circumstances or not. Circumstances are never running for public office. Like the elements, they are free of concern.

Yet each individual has to face these things somehow. By the way, the individual didn't ask for all of these *mental powers and he would rather live a child's life than that of an adult. As long as he is in a child's world, he can imagine at full blast and not have to think about the consequences. But once he becomes an adult, the consequences are real and his part in them is equally real. That is why there is such a love of the primitive in the modern age: it allows you to worship the imagination and continue running from the burden of intellect. We all can imagine. Whether what we imagine amounts to good imagining or not is no hindrance to the process. We all cannot think, or we do not all **wish** to think.*

*Ours, however, is an unprecedented era in that self-consciousness is no longer the province of the educated few but the province of the many. At no time in the history of the world has any group had such wide-open access to facts and stories and studies and so forth, from here and from the world over. There again America is unique. People have never been shut up in themselves with so much **mind** at their disposal. Of course, everybody now sees himself as a thinking person but he doesn't have the power to do much with all the thought because so much of it comes from outside, not from within. I just see us as turkeys with a stuffing of thought. That is where the question of taste becomes a serious thing. That is, what will we amount to on the palate of history?*

SAUL BELLOW,
DECEMBER 1, 2001

ADDRESSING A MASTERWORK

What Saul Bellow has achieved in his most recent novel, *Ravelstein*, is a level of control that seems absolutely spontaneous. The reader is given the experience that writers so often describe. It seems as though everything in the novel forces itself forward, as though there is no writer; or as though one is actually listening to someone talk in the way that most do when going on about others, which is to say that they never start at the start and end at the end. Homer began his tales in midstream and went on to let us know how we got to the place where we are before going on to finish off what he had to say. That is how many epics begin, and that is what *Ravelstein* is, an epic in economical space, the tale of a civilization. Like all epics, the novel raises or attempts to answer the question central to all human communities: What does it mean to be civilized?

Civilization in a democratic context—an *American* democratic context—demands writing and rewriting because humanity unbound is always good for ongoing surprises. For one thing, we must always be prepared to reconsider who's smart and who's stupid. Like Ralph Ellison, Bellow believes that brilliance can arrive from anywhere and woe to the one who underestimates (or overestimates) those at the bottom or in the middle or at the top. Every station of life wears the masks of comedy and tragedy, compassion and hatred, creation and destruction, love and hate, the substantial and the flimsy. Class does not obviate intelligence or guarantee it. Each individual is a single issue but part of a wild society that, like a child, loves to destroy its toys and attempt to rebuild them, sometimes in bizarre combinations; our national bird might more appropriately be a duck-billed platypus. All one needs is the will and the training to make the most of upward mobility, which might have nothing to do with money or power but with the expansion of the life of the mind and the feelings. That is the essence of democratic perception.

Democratic perception is the backup chorus underlining the central theme of *Ravelstein*—appetite, its riches and its dangers. To achieve his theme and to bring forward how appetite, democratic perception, and tragedy intersect, Bellow uses a protean language that obviates the distances between high and low in recognition of the social fact that an American does not require a pedigree to be in the know at both ends. Nor does an American have to have come up from the streets to have a human sense of them. *Ravelstein* tells us that the most complete expression of American freedom results in being able to move the distance from the alley to the academy and *back*. How to maintain coordination of what one has come to understand becomes the point. As a Bellow character might say, "Man takes a huge step backward when he fails to understand that he can't eat with his ass and shit with his mouth."

Bellow's central character, Abe Ravelstein, is a consumer. He has a voracious appetite for knowledge and a great capacity for absorbing it. In his position as a college professor, Ravelstein has the ability to uplift and inspire his students with the results of that appetite. As a homosexual who lived in the faceless world of brief erotic encounters that were so available before the great plague—in the bath houses, the parks, and the many other places where homosexuals lived their intense but unattached sexual lives—he is dying of AIDS. The teller of Ravelstein's tale, a writer named Chick, comes close to death through appetite as well, by ingesting some bad fish—half-cooked—in the Caribbean.

The two of them form circles. They are turns of the mind made literary. At the beginning of the book, Chick is constantly circling Ravelstein, who is himself ever turning. With each turn, we get more information about him and what he does and how he has come to be the esteemed and wealthy figure that he is. Structurally, the novel is formed of three sections with subdivisions—seven in the first part, eight in the second, seven in the third—that arrive by association or set up thematic territory, images, and words that will be returned to as Chick uses this method to tell Ravelstein's story "piecemeal," as he calls it. It is actually a way of manhandling time so that he can describe Ravelstein, speak for himself, have dialogues with his subject, and tell us his own story, which echoes elements of Ravelstein's.

This means that Chick will take over the tale—as when he introduces and tells the story of his dragon lady ex-wife or his hospital experience after food poisoning. When we have almost forgotten Ravelstein for a while—boom, he reappears in his future Boswell's recollection and reasserts himself. He is always turning Chick into a straight man, whether for funny stories or tales of woe or discussions of anti-Semitism or death or love. All of the stories apply to the behavior of his appointed biographer, and what Ravelstein makes of how Chick responds to the world and the curve balls that fate pitches at him, trying to strike out the man, the artist, the Jew.

By the end of the book, when the themes have been developed on many different planes, all adjusted to function in the complex of technology and mass production and mass appetite equaled by mass longing that is our world, Ravelstein and Chick are walking together and Abe is gesturing because he is drowned out by feral Quaker parrots that are keeping up a racket as they eat berries. Introduced on page 141 as irritants, then embraced by Ravelstein as "Jewish," and finishing in a fantasy moment of great health and sartorial splendor when the subject is at full force, the South American birds have an ability to survive in wintry Chicago that symbolizes the very improbability of Ravelstein himself. We have by then followed this man and his designated Boswell through the remarkably varied stations of life and experience an American can have both at home and abroad. We have seen the myth of upward mobility shoot Ravelstein into the millionaire zone by means of a book about American culture in decline, which the character sees as partially due to the majority of those in our academies using their tongues to swab the decks of chaotically drifting European ships of foolishly nihilistic thoughts.

There are uproariously comic scenes in which the chain-smoking Ravelstein is unable to pay the close attention necessary to maintain valuable garments or to sustain normal eating practices at a dinner table, resulting in his being an expensively dressed mess or leaving a clutter of garbage and ashes behind him. He is, like his name, a mug of ravels, of loose ends—but what wild threads! This figure of great intellectual acuity, this man so superbly gifted at making fine distinctions, at summoning up—and summing up—profound human meanings, is undone by the demon of carelessness. Ravelstein destroys himself as casually as he does an expensive jacket on which he spills food or a tie that he burns with a cigarette.

The tragedy is that the jacket or the tie is replaceable but he is not. While all human beings leave a hole when they die that cannot be filled, Ravelstein, because he is a great man, leaves a crater of memories. The point of the book is that memory might be a way of creating a perpetual succession of echoes in that crater, echoes that have the power of summoning the spirit of one who is no longer with us. Those echoes, forever rising from a landscape of such craters, form the music on which the humanity of civilization spiritually builds itself.

The rebuilding of the self through triumph over adversity (or superstition as it realizes itself in any form of bigotry) is central to the civilized impulse. In that sense, Ravelstein is a great emancipator on a smaller frame than one we are more familiar with, since "he told students that they had come to the university to learn something, and this meant that they must rid themselves of the opinions of their parents. He was going to direct them to a higher life, full of variety and diversity, governed by rationality—anything but the arid kind."

It is easy to understand the character as an emancipator, an intellectual abolitionist, since much of modern American civilization is built on what another Abraham—Lincoln—made of the democratic questions central to removing slavery, which had reduced the Declaration of Independence to toilet paper. Lincoln was the grand master of democratic perception. On the first page of the novel, Lincoln is described as one who understood the need to entertain if intent on holding the job of a democratic leader. Make them laugh. There's nothing wrong with a knee slapped now and then. There'll be plenty of time for tears. Plenty. And when war brings the tears wrought by monumental heartbreak, be ready to rally the soul of a nation so that it can understand the significance of its suffering, that it has not been in vain. Lincoln came up out of the soil, summed up the nation's troubles, engaged them, exhibited some cracker barrel wit, and died a tragic hero.

A tragic hero in death is also Ohio's Abraham Ravelstein, whose sweeping knowledge of classical philosophy and the motion of thought up, through, and beyond Nietzsche distinguishes him. His wit is a variation on Lincoln's. Ravelstein's reaches back to the Yiddish theater just as the Great Emancipator's jokes and stories pulled forward homespun yucks from the roughhewn, rail-splitting world of his youth. Lincoln was dismissed as an ape by his secretary of war, who hated his sense of humor. Democracy, entertainment, war, unsanitized wit, and the battle between science and poetry symbolized by the Scopes "Monkey" Trial are themes dropped on the reader in the first two pages, as is the death by appetite when we are told that some believed the huge Nebraska meals loved by William Jennings Bryan were fundamental to his finale. In addition, the pterodactyl is mentioned as a failed and early version of the bird.

We learn that Ravelstein—whom we first meet full of life in his kimono and meet again in the same garment later when he is dying—is a millionaire. It is an improbable kind of success, not necessarily easy to understand, that must be accepted, just as the presence of both Michael Jackson ("this glamour monkey") and Ravelstein at the Crillon in Paris must be accepted. These two visiting forces symbolize all that has happened since Jefferson and Franklin were there, since the Civil War was fought, since the Lost Generation, and since the truth of the matter is that the very size of America makes it possible, with more than a quarter of a billion potential customers (or recipients), for all manner of people to become fabulously wealthy and still fit into what are called niche markets. It is just as easy for Ravelstein to be known and remain unread as it is for Jackson to be known but not listened to yet maintain fanatic followers the world over, avid readers and listeners who number in the millions.

Ravelstein's success results from the printing press just as Jackson's draws on the recording, the radio, the television, the motion picture, and the concert, which makes use of large screens so that the multitudes out there can see him in close-up. He is placed in the novel to introduce an important theme—fascism, rock and roll, and war are now media events, like sports. The challenge that remains, forever, is just how much humanity arrives through our machinery.

Or how much information. Ravelstein carries a cell phone and hears from ex-students who are among decision makers during the Gulf War, or he is given stock market tips, or he keeps a credit card that makes sure, daily, that he gets the best rate of exchange while in Paris. In that City of Light, Ravelstein is surrounded by every kind of reference to high culture, World Wars I and II, fashion, and food. He is among descendants of the people whom Julius Caesar described as panting lovers of new things even two thousand years ago. Fashion-fixated Gauls.

He also finds himself in a place that reverberates with the two most important secondary themes: betrayal and loyalty. The highly cultured French, for all of their grand talk, essentially betrayed the Jews during World War II and even provided the Germans with the language of the Third Reich in the Dreyfus trial (1894). Scattered among the wonderful French pastries and marvelous chocolates are hard, poisonous candies. In fact, European civilization betrayed the Jews, as it later betrayed the people of Bosnia.

Like the French, the millions of other Europeans who submitted to anti-Semitism, and the American academy that sold out its grasp of the grand tradition to identity politics and European nihilism, Chick's wife, Vela, is a betrayer, a brilliant figure in the world of chaos physics. Her branch of math clearly symbolizes the amoral relationship that math and science have had to death camp experiments, biological warfare, and "weapons of mass destruction," as our politicians now call them. (Yet it is the moral use of scientifically derived medical information and technology that saves Chick at the end.) Vela is a chilled beauty full of devotion to figures but uninterested in people other than those who can bolster her career or sexually service her outside of her marriage. Vela hates Ravelstein but Chick is loyal to him. Rosamund, Chick's next wife, is so loyal to her husband that she brings him back to the world of the living after he was poisoned in a lovely St. Martin setting "by the red snapper set before me by Bedier, a tough guy playing the Frenchiest of French hosts." Had by the Gauls again!

In Chicago, Ravelstein is a Bulls fan whose soul is polished by the genius of Michael Jordan. Ravelstein observes, while passing out slices of delivered pizza to his students at NBA parties held in front of his television, that jazz and basketball are two Negro contributions to the higher levels of American culture. Basketball players have become as important to our society as bullfighters in Spain or tenors in Ireland. Moving up from the Civil War, Ravelstein tells Chick how impressed he is by the black military men during the Gulf War, so well spoken and so technologically masterful. Aware of how oddly we Americans line up in taste and information, Abe finds it ironic that while his academic colleagues have no idea what he is wearing, Negro kids on the street stop him and knowingly discuss his sartorial splendor. On every level, Ravelstein is a man whose appetite is for integration—across time, across class, across color lines, across nations, and so on and on. His is a perfectly realized version of democratic man fusing with serious intellectual.

Few characters in contemporary fiction have been drawn as vividly, and few living writers could summon such a liberated form while maintaining coherence. Saul Bellow does a marvelous job of fooling us into believing, at first, that the repetitions are mistakes rather than the masterful simulating of how one tells a tale in actual life—saying things, repeating them with extensions, circling back to subjects over and over as more parts are recalled and more must be said in order to make things truly clear. After all, clarity is the high road to lyricism, which remains never less than mysterious. That is why *Ravelstein*, finally, is a lyrical mystery and a compact epic that summons up a civilization in the way that only a grand master can, which is to say in a superbly original way. The mystery yields to a few observations about what it means to be civilized, however: one needs to be loyal to the highest principles of human commonality raised by the Enlightenment; one has to be willing to bring back from the dead those people most important to our living world, and one may be tested when called on for the kind of self-sacrifice that involves saving someone who is barely among the living but, given the right spiritual support, can be born again by making a womb of the mouth of death.

Have a taste. You'll love it.

Blues at the Top

LAST WEEK ON HBO, DENNIS MILLER QUIPPED THAT IT was quite a brave and selfless act for a white superstar like Michael Jackson to speak up about injustices against black people in the recording industry. Mr. Miller went on to say that Mr. Jackson should stop bitching about racism at the top of the recording industry as if that explained why so few units of his recent *Invincible* album sold. The moonwalker, he said, should just accept being over the hill. Mr. Miller pointed out, as have others, that most young fans of pop music these days weren't even conscious when Mr. Jackson began his climb to unprecedented success—his 1982 album *Thriller* is one of the top two highest-selling albums in the history of recorded sound—some twenty years ago.

To stop there, however, would be naive. No matter how eccentric Michael Jackson is, no matter how self-serving his charges might seem, he is reviving an old story, full of exploited figures, that is still very much alive. Among the lessons of his rise and fall from grace is a cold hard fact that black artists and entertainers have to grow up and realize: in show business nothing is guaranteed, regardless of the color of the person making the promise.

Speaking from the Reverend Al Sharpton's National Action Network offices, Mr. Jackson charged that the recording business is racist and that his case is about the essential nature of color prejudice. "If you're fighting for me, you're fighting for all black people, dead and alive," Mr. Jackson claimed. His troubles, he said, resulted from Sony's policy of trying to hold him back. He called Sony Music chairman Tommy Mottola a racist and a "devil" who privately describes certain black artists as "niggers." Mr. Jackson also asserted that his many media scandals are part of a conspiracy to keep him from sustaining the power that, by all rights, should come with breaking the records of Elvis Presley and the Beatles. His career, according to Mr. Jackson, is nothing but a contemporary version of all that has happened to black people in the music business since recordings started bringing in big money and the exploitation of black performers and composers began.

Here Mr. Jackson is not riding his horse backward. American music, from the buffoon minstrelsy of the nineteenth century to the thug-and-slut minstrelsy of gangster rap, has been strongly influenced by black people. The blues craze of the 1920s led to the drive to record Negro artists such as Bessie Smith—and also built what is now Sony. In fact, in an ongoing pattern, Negro musicians have been cheated and left behind as the industry moved on to the next trend. This is the black part of an icy show business reality that applies to all who don't look closely enough at their contracts or outlive their usefulness. (White actresses know all about it too.)

But however hard black people in show business have it, it's harder still for many to buy Mr. Jackson's conclusion. The facts of Mr. Jackson's case seem to be more about green than black or white. *Billboard* reported that *Invincible* cost $30 million to make and that Sony invested $25 million in promotion and refused to continue once sales turned out to be sluggish—only 5.1 million units worldwide. The reason for the extraordinary production costs is that Mr. Jackson took a long time to finish the project. Industry insiders told me that the artist, ever sensitive to environmental vibrations, had asked to have three recording studios available around the clock so that he could work on the East Coast, in the Midwest, or in California, depending on how he felt. If the singer's feeling compelled him to travel, this apparently meant first-class plane tickets for him and his entourage as well as ground transportation and accommodations.

Sony is alleged to have made a $55 million loan against Mr. Jackson's catalog, which, according to industry contacts, is worth about $1 billion and includes the music of the Beatles, a treasure the singer outbid Paul McCartney, among others, to land.

People inside the industry say that the real deal is this: Sony tried to bust a move on Mr. Jackson that would have resulted in the company owning that catalog. Mr. Jackson publicly called the company out, and they backed down and negotiated another financial resolution.

While a battle for a billion-dollar music catalog between a black artist and a record company is worth looking into, Mr. Jackson has long muddied the waters on simple definitions of color and culture. He was accused of hating himself and trying to "look white" when he began to change his appearance in a radical way. The changes were supposed to be career moves that would take him farther into America as a brand-new white man.

Actually, he seems to be turning himself into a flesh and blood Disney cartoon character, with the lighter skin, the turned-up nose, the falling hair that can be thrown back.

Yet in this land of nose jobs, trimmed-down ears, breast reductions, breast implants, gluteal implants, penile implants, liposuction, skin bleaching, tanning spas, and the rest of it, Michael Jackson is no more than a neon extreme. Had he taken steroids, gone to the gym, and become monstrously overdeveloped, the singer would have been in the same lane. As for racial identity, he is no less absurd than your run-of-the-mill yellow or bone-colored West Indian black nationalist academic telling you how purely African he is in his soul and how you should let him tell you, the Negro American, how to be black.

At the same time, Mr. Jackson was celebrated among black people for the commercial success that outstripped nearly everyone else. Regardless of all that was repulsive or confusing about him, the pop star made up symbolically for all of the Negro musicians who had been used and abused, whose material had been taken by an industry that reprocessed it with white stars and excluded the originators from the victory party of high profits, and for all the black men and women who never became film stars in roles other than servants.

There are also black people who argue that Mr. Jackson became successful because his androgynous manner didn't threaten white men—while brute masculine rappers with gold teeth and drooping pants occupy the other end of the Negro Freak Show for White Folks.

Mr. Jackson exemplified the burgeoning rise of a black upper class—Negroes worth millions of dollars, creating billions in profit and creeping ever closer to the punch line of a recent joke: "Who wants to be a millionaire? Everybody. *Except* a billionaire." Recently Bob Johnson, the creator of Black Entertainment Television (BET), became the nation's first black billionaire, and others such as Oprah Winfrey and Michael Jordan, given solid investment, should eventually scale that wall. In Mr. Jackson's case, there was also his short-lived marriage to Elvis Presley's daughter, in one of our laughable versions of aristocracy (which is supposed to distinguish mere wealth from refinement), a quality that characterized neither the bride nor the groom—who was happiest, it appeared, in the company of his chimpanzee. Mr. Jackson had climbed the ladder of material success but ended up at a great remove from any ethnic group or class other than the extremely wealthy, who live with a level of privilege that is closer to fantasy than the reality of most of the human race.

Mr. Jackson is part of the group who proved that being black and being successful does not mean literally or symbolically getting beyond the universal demons that have brought many of the race down. The sexual scandals he found himself in the middle of linked Mr. Jackson to O.J. Simpson, Marion Barry, Mike Tyson, Suge Knight, Tupac Shakur, and Biggie Smalls, not one of whom adhered to a social script written by the Boy Scouts of America. Some compared themselves to spiritual maggots climbing from the project garbage cans of the nation, where they lived the thug life.

A black man with national connections in the business world once said to me of Mr. Jackson's new identity as a race leader, "The consensus in black America is right message, *wrong* messenger. That's half the people; the other half feels that if the brother wants to come back home, let him come on in. He touched many people at Sharpton's place up in Harlem when he said that he had grown up worshiping James Brown, Wilson

Pickett, and Jackie Wilson, and that he had gone on to sell more records than anyone in history, and that he had been accused of bleaching his skin, of being a homosexual and a pedophile; but when he looks in the mirror, he sees a proud black man."

The real issue, then, is not Mr. Jackson, proud or not proud, bleached or not bleached, homosexual or heterosexual or pedophile or not. "The real issue," as one industry person told me, "is how racist the recording industry is, which can easily be seen by noticing that there are fewer black people with any kind of executive authority or power in the recording industry than anywhere else in corporate America." There are political implications as well: "This is a very big issue for the Democrats because, under Clinton, the Democratic Party sold itself to Hollywood, which meant that it came to rely on the most racist industry in the country. If the Republicans were able to rise up out of their own racism—which is doubtful, given the fact that they were never able to listen to J.C. Watts and make any kind of serious overtures to black Americans—they could put some real heat on the Democratic Party's presentation of itself as the only friend of the national black community."

That is a profound point. Others I have spoken with in the world of business and entertainment observe that all over America we can find black people on the boards of major corporations: the automobile industry (which black people consider the most open), consumer-goods boards, financial institutions (such as Fannie Mae and Merrill Lynch), and even the oil industry, which tends, historically, to be among the worst.

One record industry insider said, "Look, Michael Jackson is complaining about how they did him because he had his 'nigger moment.' He found out that he was still a nigger, no matter how many records he had sold all over the world. He was still a nigger to *them*. That means some simple things, because you never have anybody in a high position to really get your back. They take your marketing budget and they charge it off against what you owe them. But they keep the money among themselves. They don't even *think* about spreading it among *us*. Wal-Mart has a black advertising agency among those it has given contracts to; so have General Motors, Ford, Microsoft, Verizon Wireless, Anheuser-Busch, Citibank, American Airlines, Toyota, McDonald's, Coca-Cola, PepsiCo. The record industry has a higher percentage of product bought by black folk than any industry. But they have so much contempt for the black community that they don't feel that they have to hire black professionals to do *any* of their work in the business area. They further demonstrate contempt for the community by putting out product which glorifies misogyny, violence, drug abuse, alcohol abuse, and other anti-social behavior that is not representative of 95 percent of black Americans. If you take them a good product, they won't give you a record deal. Trent Lott has a more integrated staff meeting than Tommy Mottola has at Sony—and Trent Lott doesn't even pretend to be a friend of black folk. Though I imagine he might have been willing to marry Mariah Carey, too."

Some wonder if, even though Mr. Mottola is Italian, Mr. Jackson's battle is no more than a coded version of the conflict between black entertainers and Jewish executives in the recording business. Black-Jewish conflict is an old favorite, but I find it odd that so much is made of the many Jews at high levels in the music or movie business. Any mention of this is supposed to be an anti-Semitic remark.

I don't get it. Jews seem to run most of the entertainment business—but you're talking about no more than fifty to a hundred people in top executive positions, almost all of whom would no doubt cut the throats of the rest for larger market shares. After all, they are in *business*, and the world of business,

no matter the religious background or ethnic culture of the players, can warm you one moment and freeze you out the next.
Besides that, Jewish executives, like black basketball players, represent far, far less than 1 percent of "their" people, since there
are 6 million Jews in America. So I don't get it. On that level.

In the case of Mr. Jackson, as always, there is another. When
Mr. Jackson's *HIStory* was released, it contained a track on
which he used the lyric "Jew me, sue me, everybody do me, /
Kick me, kike me, don't you black and white me." The song
was entitled "They Don't Care About Us," and it attempted to
both complain about Mr. Jackson's media-driven scandal and
appropriate every victim as though his blues were the same as
theirs. The Anti-Defamation League did not see it that way and
protested. Mr. Jackson apologized and promised to go into the
studio and have the second batch appear with the controver-
sial words removed.

The version that reached the street was different: a few hundred thousand units of product were snatched off the shelves.
Mr. Jackson was ordered to do another version that didn't contain the lines, and he had to hold a few press conferences swear-
ing up and down that there wasn't an anti-Semitic bone in his
callow body.

The folkloric version of the tale left some black people
seething. "These Jews don't care about all the product calling
people 'niggers' and 'bitches' and 'hos' and 'motherfuckers.'
Remember when they ran that fool Professor Griff out of Public Enemy because he was an anti-Semite? They were *right*. But
they don't care about *us*. They don't snatch that gangster-nigger
product off the shelves and make people go back in the studio,
then give press conferences apologizing."

While that might be true, it is also true that neither the
NAACP nor any other high-profile black organization has

made a sustained protest about gangster-rap words and images in the way they would had white people, Jewish or not, created, pushed, and profited from the product, as whites did during the first minstrel era. One should not naively assume that black record executives and producers such as Russell Simons or Suge Knight, or anybody else in the business who has made millions denigrating black youth, is concerned about it. As long as those words allow them to line their pockets, and as long as those videos depicting black youth as hedonistic near beasts help push product, they will make them. So complaints should be made about the *entire* business when such subjects are raised. Neither black entertainers nor black people have any automatic friends.

This blues deserves some doggerel in order to be "up to date." White might or might not be all right. Black might get your back or lead the attack. Neither trust nor distrust anyone solely on the basis of skin tone.

What is most significant about Michael Jackson and his battle with Sony is what it says about the world we're still living in. When it comes to the music industry, even those who have brought in billions—even Michael Jackson—can find himself in a position to play the race card and deserve a hearing. The denigration of black people is far from over.

Blues for the Artificial White Man

*That same year, Leonard Michaels gave a guest
workshop, discussing my (autobiographical) short story,
which was about playing on an otherwise all-black
junior high school basketball team, and Daniel's
(autobiographical) short story, which was about getting
held up by a group of black teenagers in a subway car.
Michaels explained that racism consists precisely of the
impulse to generalize, which in his opinion, both of our
stories, in their different way, did. He then asked,
"What's this thing going on here, anyway, between
Jewish men and black men." Mock-naive, as if he were
unaware that the question was a generalization.*

DAVID SHIELDS, *BLACK PLANET*

Some books are too important to let go by because of what
they tell us about where we are in ways that seem even more
startling than we might expect. When *Black Planet* by David
Shields came out a few years ago, its content was not recognized

for what it actually was. That content is nevertheless important if
we are to perceive the confounding human dimensions of our
moment as they arrive in the arenas of ethnic interplay. In that
sense, *Black Planet*, a much less serious effort than it pretends to
be, provides us with a look at just how far removed from the
arena of substantially engaged thinking the cultural issues arising
from the confusions of color and ethnic identity remain.

The book follows the Seattle SuperSonics through the entire
1994–1995 season in the National Basketball Association. It is a
day-by-day journal in which the writer gives us his version of the
subtitle, "Facing Race During an NBA Season." Shields presents
himself as a suburban Virgil leading us into what he considers the
frenzied dreamworld of other white men like himself, whose
hearts, hopes, and fantasies rise and fall with the fortunes of basketball teams dominated by black men. Shields believes that
something essential about our country is found in that set of real-
and dreamworld relationships. Much of it, according to him, has
to do with being—or not being—what he calls "cool." He writes,
with the appropriate self-loathing and envy that defines so much
of the text, "For white guys, for millions of white guys including
myself who are not cool!!, watching basketball is one last chance
if not to be cool at least to get in contact with cool."

But is Shields just another faceless white guy, or is he an artificial white man whose refusal to address his own ethnic identity
removes nuance and possible insight from the book? The autobiographical *Remote*, the book Shields wrote before *Black Planet*,
is a loose, occasionally interesting commentary on American
celebrity. It is written from the standpoint of his adult reflec-
tions on himself as a pimply, smart, stuttering Jewish youth who
had a good basketball game but always felt like an outsider. His
oblique relationship to popular culture and the Jewish role in it
are considered again and again. In *Black Planet*, Shields makes

nothing of his Jewishness or the complexity it adds to his psychological relationship to black men in basketball shorts. In *Remote*, he writes (as if preparing the way for questions never raised in *Black Planet)*, "In movies, Jewish characters can be many things—wits, cowards, whiners, geniuses, villains, accountants—but they are never one thing: the embodiment of the life force, who is always an Italian."

Is this really true, especially after Woody Allen? In the context of romantic comedy, Allen radically rearranged the look and the background of an American leading man to include the bookish, witty, unhandsome guy; bourgeois masculinity proved itself most vital in the talking and physical elements of romance. Backgrounded by long walks and plenty of conversations that poked holes in modern anxieties, this masculinity was almost always sexual, private. In the bedroom a man was not held to the public standard of chest puffing or muscle flexing, drinking himself senseless, or bloodying others while being bloodied himself. Allen rejected the animal side of public masculinity, went past "gentile beefcake," as Pauline Kael wrote of him, and broadened our vision of masculinity in a way that, as Kael continued, made him "a new national hero." His characters were distinctly Jewish—New York Jewish—and they lived in Manhattan. They won and lost attractive women, most of them non-Jewish, some of whom were bundles of sizzling, unmatched wires; others were hot, foxy, bright, and charming but usually overwhelmed, as were Allen's characters generally, by their own neuroses. The interplay between Woody Allen's men and the women with whom they were involved was another version of the ongoing integration that is the downbeat of the American day.

This is not good enough for Shields. He wants us to feel enlightened as he writes about the underlying inadequacies of white men who rarely possess memories of themselves as athletes but live out imagined athletic lives as they go bonk-the-bonk-bonkers over the dribbling and passing and stealing and shooting of Negroes who are largely illiterate, are often rude, and tend to live in a secret world concealed from their audience of admirers, the overwhelming majority of whom are not black in skin tone but are in their favorite dreams. As our would-be Virgil fidgets in the suburbs of Seattle, any close reader quickly realizes that these basketball players symbolize his hatred of a schoolteacher's bourgeois life, filled with endless quiet, the unfair, soul-draining demands of grading papers, a Christian wife from suburban Chicago who might not actually be as dull as he presents her, and a daughter who is given plenty of attention but little of the emotion he reserves for those shadow figures with rubber balls.

The writer is suffocated by his easy life and the well-meaning but exaggerated courtesy of Seattle, which he responds to with the teenage emotion that produces broken windows, flattened tires, and small fires—the angst of troubled boys who have not become men. In the process, the perspective of the book confuses bad boys with those who have the most individual freedom. We should not, therefore, be surprised by Shields's awestruck reactions, which back up out of the cultural commode and have the smell of the most anarchic rock and the conventional amorality of gangster rap.

Disdain for manners is a driving force in this book. The black people Shields claims to appreciate most are not those who are well spoken or carry themselves with an ease that is confident but not confrontational. With the apparent exception of retired basketball titan Bill Russell, those refined Negroes, in his opinion, are too concerned with making white people feel "comfortable." They have sold themselves to white convention and are intimidated into good behavior. Shields prefers the sort with the least regard for white people, what have been called "white standards," and any kind of deportment other than that of the distant, the cryptic, the aboriginal. The Negro who "talks trash" excites the writer because this purportedly expresses a concern with "language." Of a player whose secondary gift besides basketball skill is the willingness to sustain a yammering harassment of his opposing players, Shields writes, "[His] game is better than anyone else's because his language is better than anyone else's. My identification with him is total." The black American's greatest refinements are expressed not in medicine, science, education, the arts, and technology, but in shorts, tennis shoes, and a sleeveless jersey, "talking trash" on the polished hardwood of a basketball court, sort of a flattened bush where primordial updates are available to the eye. Shields attacks this tendency in himself and others to reduce black men to athletic flesh held in place by the meat hooks of Caucasian projections. But, like a blacksmith addicted to making the same form over and over, he continues to forge new meat hooks and hoist these men into place.

After he details his preference for the stage savagery of athletic knotheads, the writer tells us that he imagines being Gary Payton, the player who had his foot on the gas pedal of the Seattle SuperSonics when the book was written: "I'm not him. I'm really not him. I wish I were him. I love him—the phantasm of him—to death." Shields is inspirationally drilled to the quick by Payton's refusal to play the part of a nice guy who puts white people at ease. He loves to see Payton string along white sports reporters or ignore their questions or use a counterfeit illiteracy that he brings into the skin tone game as a way of toying with white fantasies about his own ignorance. As Shields observes, "He seems near-phobic to me about making sure he doesn't say two correct words consecutively."

In *Soul on Ice,* Eldridge Cleaver wrote that Elvis Presley "gave the white man his body back" through his swiveling hips, a frenzied display of undiluted rutting intentions. Presley presented a savage male libido backed up by the amateurish rhythms and teenage passions of rock and roll. The King of Rock and Roll let loose the sexual fire of the white male held down by middle-class niceties. Payton and other black men do more than this for the writer of *Black Planet.* The mere thought of them on the plantation of dreams aids Shields in harvesting an orgasm instead of a crop. One night, instead of making love to his wife, Shields "fucks" her as he imagines a black man would. On another night, he envisions himself as Payton when he and his wife get naked and do the nasty. On yet another, unable to achieve orgasm, he thinks about Charles Barkley going to strip clubs and arrives, finally, at sweet release. Hmm.

We know it could not stop there. This book is not about brown sex aids. It is about what Payton represents to Shields. The Payton drawn on these pages seems to have no respect for anything other than his playing ability, his personal life, and his career. This makes him more than perfect for Shields's purpose, providing the writer with an indefectible escape from the strictures of genteel manners recast in a hippie-derived West Coast frame. That social frame includes a supposedly vacuous geniality that the writer battles by being as rude and obnoxious in public as he can, making the teenage subtext of his own life clear. Shields drops this subtext into the very low hoop of the book:

> In and around Seattle, you see kids wearing not only Sonics jerseys . . . but also jerseys of players from other teams— almost always guys who not only are great players but have a *fuck you attitude* . . . Today, for instance, because for some reason there seems to be an amazing number of kids walking

around wearing NBA jerseys, you can feel with a certain clarity what the whole thing is about: how much of these kids' swagger comes from the players, the sheer volume of hope/possibility/resistance these guys represent. Is it just my imagination, or does even Natalie [his daughter] raise more hell than usual when she's wearing her Sonics outfit?

The immaturity expressed in this passage is heightened in the overall terrain of the book because it is the result of a *willful* adolescence, not the helpless hell-raising of a person so poorly educated or underdeveloped that experience is never assessed beyond the perspectives of a teenage boy. For Shields, "fuck you attitudes" and "cool" are the ultimate achievements and amount to qualities that black men such as Gary Payton have, of course, in spades. Yet one wonders why Shields, who teaches writing in the English Department at the University of Washington, does not recognize this quality as related to Hemingway's "grace under pressure" or the British "stiff upper lip" or the menacing relaxation of the Asian martial arts master or the toreador's ability to remain calm and focused, even when the horns of the bull have torn his tight pants and grazed or cut his thighs in the process. The reason is simple and acidic. Shields does not perceive black Americans in the realm of humanity at large. He tries but finds it impossible. They exist primarily as blackboards on which the chalk of white fantasies are forever moving. As he writes, "We came to see Dennis Rodman act like a nut and we were disappointed . . . we come to see Scottie Pippen throw chairs and we are disappointed again . . . We pretend we want them to be controlled and 'classy,' but really what we them to do is misbehave, so we can equate their talent with inadequacy, reaffirming their deep otherness, their mad difference." That is a somewhat provocative look at a ritual Shields claims is defined by a "mixture of reverence and contempt." It is a central theme of the book but is far from sufficient, for more than a few reasons.

What about his *own* "deep otherness," his *own* "mad difference"? Shields makes nothing of his own "peasant stock," as he calls it, and how it fits into the overall ethnic mix that complicates the question of identity, which is always fraudulent when the false simplicity of "black and white" is assumed to say it all. Shields tickle-toes the deep end of the pool but never jumps in. He mentions fiction he has written about white men wanting to be black, about his own experience growing up and playing basketball with white guys who disliked his style. They disliked aspects of it that made him too much like a black player. Young Shields drew pleasure from angering them. Why? Were the white guys who criticized Shields's basketball style Jews? If so, what did their disdain for his approach to the game mean to him and how did their attitude fit into the overall interplay, absorption, remaking, and rejection of styles that determine the protean feeling of American life? If not, what did it mean among Christian amateurs? Was he too aggressive, too selfish, too devoid of sportsmanship, like a disturbing number of the professional black athletes we see today? No reader of *Black Planet* will ever know.

Shields makes no comment when recalling a writing workshop where Leonard Michaels, a fellow Jew, tried to nudge him into publicly contemplating those kinds of meaning by asking him about the fascination with Negroes shown in his short fiction. That Shields chose to duck the question is more than odd, especially since Jews' relationships to black Americans are full of intricacy and offer a serious writer much to examine. These relationships involve political alliances, high culture, artist management, the recording industry, both racist and liberal images in cinema and television, issues of romance as well as marriage, and so on and on. Jews have done everything from discovering, managing, promoting, and exploiting Negroes to dying with them side by side in Mississippi during the civil rights movement. Their involvement with Negroes in basketball extends from Abe Saperstein's belittling, paternal control of the clowning Harlem Globetrotters, all the way over to David Stern's wise stewardship of the National Basketball Association. Stern has actually suspended certain black players for throwing aside all sportsmanship and acting like thugs and asses.

But this material is not interesting enough and the context is not small enough for Shields. He prefers to pretend he is sitting on the insider's bench. This allows him to take to the microphone in the role of Mr. White Everyman as though Jews (unlike the Irish and the Italians) didn't have to work through the disparaging ethnic exotica imposed on them in order to become "real" white people. The decision to "pass for white" airbrushes away the ethnic resentment that certain Jews—from the blue-collar bottom to the upper-class top—feel toward what one author called "the ordeal of civility." The fused arguments and discontents that Shields falls on, like a sword, have precedents going back to French intellectuals and artists such as Rousseau, de Sade, Baudelaire, and Rimbaud (who tellingly spoke of a "love of sacrilege"). The 1894 Dreyfus trial in France raised many questions about the role of prejudice in Christian culture and society. Reactions ranging from brilliant to petty attend discourse that beams in on anti-Semitism and the ambiguous threats at the center of hate and superstition. The thrust has usually been to accept as human those who do not fit the conventional (and sometimes demanded!) profile. Arguments for freedom from provincialism have used Marx, Freud, sociology, cultural anthropology, medicine, statistics, and whatever else might be available to shatter the entrapments of stereotypes. These Jewish reassessments of convention, order, and "normality" may have been trying at first, especially since the wheat and the chaff must be separated. But the most telling of those reassessments have benefited all in the modern world and are essential to dismantling xenophobia and continually redefining American democracy.

In the process of this reassessment, the blandness of the middle class, supposedly the world's safest place for all who can get there, has been repeatedly attacked and its puritanical timbers have been shaken. Here is where Shields comes in. He hates being middle-class because he believes its purported hollow ritual, coldness, and overweening sweetness puncture and destroy all aspirations to adventure. Shields is not one who believes, as Irving Howe said in *The World of Our Fathers,* that Jewish vulgarity brought a vitality to the suburbs because it stripped away pretentiousness. Shields is not that observant or imaginative. He misses one of the grand intellectual challenges of our time because he has no alternative vision of middle-class vitality. There is no attempt to analyze what Jews and others *may* have lost in the transition from the peasantry to the bourgeoisie. Shields has no idea how that lost vibrancy might be reborn as a way of facing life that could provide *richer* ways of resisting exterior boredom and sterility than retreating into adolescence. There is a reason for this. Sacrilege moves the writer most. Part of his admiration of Gary Payton is made specific when he writes that "he's as bad as we'd like to be, if we ever got good at being bad."

Because his eyes are ever focused away from the deeper details of his own life and the lives of others suffering the foam rubber slings and arrows of middle-class living, we know little about this remarkably narcissistic man beyond his childish obsessions. Have the white folks gotten so cozy and so melted down in the gruel of the bourgeoisie that Jewish or Christian, Catholic or Protestant no longer have *any* distinctions? What does celebrating Christmas with the narrator's sister-in-law mean? Or do these family holidays, founded in very different religious backgrounds and perhaps very different ethnic subcultures, now have no meaning, only different days? Do the grandparents of the daughter born to Shields and his Christian wife care about *her* religious identity? Is the life lived by Shields an example of cultural schizophrenia or a broader embrace of what is available, since individuals and their backgrounds come together in a marriage?

Shields is so at ease in his version of cultural investigation that, other than some dull sexual notes, we are offered no insights into the cultural compounds of his home. Does the sometimes perplexing condition of ethnic identity that Philip Roth describes in *American Pastoral*—when the Jewish guy marries the Irish gal—apply, *in any way*, to Shields and his wife? We can only wonder, since her humanity is never as important as her bedroom availability, her feather-heavy opinions, and the fact that she also has an erotic dream about Gary Payton. The closest Shields gets to complexity is found in two instances. In the first, arguing—almost beyond comprehension—for his ethnicity *and* his artificiality, he writes, "On the first night of Chanukah, Laurie and I have another ridiculous debate as to whether Natalie's hair is blonde (WASP) or brown (Jewish)... [Laurie] wants her to be a seraph... and my fantasy is for Natalie to become a bad girl. (James Baldwin wrote, 'When you call yourself white, you force me to call myself black.')" In the second, Shields describes being repulsed by a minor exhibition of bad manners when his father visits: "I'm lashing out at my peasant stock, I suppose, but I'm also situating myself on an evolutionary scale: I'm not as 'civilized' as Laurie (with her blonde hair and good manners), but I'm more 'civilized' than my father (with his dirty sweater and Brooklyn accent)." This is a signal example of how Shields both addresses his Jewishness and evades it. He is saying that his manners are not as refined as those of his wife, whose blonde hair somehow matches her degree of civilization. That's a good one. Would Shields have better manners or be more inclined to civilized behavior if he were blond? Might his daughter, whose only chance is being a bad girl and having dark hair? Outside of a bottle, how many white women *actually* have blonde hair, and does their identity as WASPS become less distinct as their hair darkens? We cannot be sure. But this writer, if we accept his claim, is better at handling the "ordeal of civility" than his father is. The weightless barbarism of Pop Shields is made clear to us by the dirt on his sweater and his accent. Apparently Pop, as is to be expected of those less evolved, has been permanently damaged by the darker hair. Pop remains the child of the ones just off the boat, a man whose unaware abrasiveness includes the telltale *Jewish* version of the Brooklyn accent (there are Irish, Italian, and Negro versions as well). There you have it.

There is another cultural issue that is often obscured. Shields thinks of black people only in terms of slavery and racism or the extraordinary salaries in the NBA, which he assumes are part of an unacknowledged gesture of reparations for the hard times had by their people over the past five hundred years. This is ridiculous. Athletes get as much as they do because the owners of teams can afford the salaries. Like moviemakers, owners pay for talent because they are *forced to* by negotiating agents and because the presence of those players on the court is necessary for profit. Another serious intellectual shortcoming holds firm, regardless of Shields's slavish drooling in his pursuit of the alienated but triumphant black athlete: there is no contemplation of how deeply rooted in Americana the Negro actually is. We can consider that only when we get past the cultural lawn jockey of the black man as mere nature boy. The immigrant tradition shared by so many avid white sports fans that Shields portrays, whether Christian or Jewish, is not as deep a part of American history, from the top of the seventeenth century through the Civil War, as that shared by Negroes and British Isles whites. Negroes dramatically influenced everything in America—the law, the food, the music, the humor, the architecture, the rodeo, the dance, the technology—and helped define, as Constance Rourke observed, the particular qualities that we refer to as American.

The crude simplicity of "black and white" limits the writer's thinking. He has misgivings about the shortcomings of bourgeois American life and never fails to sneer at them or rant about their unsatisfying qualities. But Shields never wonders about the propelling vision of those he celebrates for assuming an attack mode on the way of life he has chosen for himself and for his family. The writer never wonders if black Americans, having prevailed against the irony of bigoted exclusion for so long, are perhaps experiencing an unprecedented rise while suffering from an equally unprecedented fall into decadence, self-destructive behavior, and despair. Is the worst of what we can see the best of what we can expect of knotheads who have left high-mindedness behind them in unapologetic pursuit of mammon? Has the strength of Negro American culture been replaced by a scowling shrunken head shaped by the culture's elevation of the narcissism at the center of irresponsible and criminal behavior—the "fuck you attitude" that makes Shields cream in his jeans? Was a certain stratum of black Americans affected in exactly the opposite direction intended by Francis Ford Coppola and Brian de Palma in the *Godfather* series and

Scarface, inspiring the deification of Michael Corleone and Tony Montana, characters of iconic status among rappers, black street thugs, and would-be thugs?

These are serious questions that go way beyond Shields's version of "facing race." As a writer, he reveals no sense of moral consideration or intellectual depth coming from Negroes. Yes, he is critical of the fantasy use of Negroes, his own and that of other whites, but this man evidently never read or spoke to Negroes with brains who would challenge his narrow description of black people—all meat, all fantasy, all rhythm, all bad behavior at their most admirable. The arguments raised by thinkers such as Ralph Ellison, Albert Murray, and Charles Johnson have gone right past him. This is very odd for a teacher at a university, where there must be black colleagues who can take on these issues. Consequently Shields is at an even greater distance from black people of intelligence than he is from successful boys on the court. He is incapable of assessing how little black Americans have gained by rejecting everything about this nation other than money, status, and power. The irony deepens as we consider how the oppositional ideas of Malcolm X and Franz Fanon decayed into blaxploitation and the elevation of "the street brother," who eventually became the rapper, the first biker parallel in Afro-American history—an apolitical, illiterate roughneck who titillated middle-class black girls and helped destroy the taste and the intellectual engagement of far too many black boys across the country.

In his fantasy world, Shields is too busy "getting his." He cannot travel past the acceptance of atrocious behavior within a unique area of American entertainment. After all, bad boy athletes represent something indisputably real, and that blinds him to everything else. Unlike movie stars or any other entertainers, they face *actual* victory and defeat, not symbolic versions. They have spurned the rules of the nice guy in the way that James Cagney did as Tom Powers in *Public Enemy*—except, of course, Cagney was acting. While the most unruly and repulsive black athletes have been accepted as chocolate-dipped bad boys, that is true of very few Jewish careers in the straight and icy world of legitimate business, scholarship, and entertainment (though the Jewish bull in the china shop reached a nadir in the work of Lenny Bruce and the bottom of the tar pits in Andrew Dice Clay's sorry imitation of a foul-mouthed black comedian). Still, Shields, wrapped in his self-referential cocoon, needs something bigger, a transcendent celebrity. This allows him to push the love of sports into the heavens as he identifies with what he considers the meaning of fundamentalist Christianity: "They go to church for the same reason fans go to games: adulthood didn't turn out to have quite as much glory as we thought it would; for an hour or two, we're in touch with transcendental things." Ah so. But could it be possible that black people at the bottom need more than the hour or two experienced by this Jewish writer who followed his own tradition of hard study and hard work into the very middle class he disdains?

One of those "transcendental things" is how black athletes, refusing to repress their lack of manners and grace, sacked Rome and were celebrated for it. Shields alludes to this whenever he writes of Payton imitating the laugh of Snoop Doggy Dogg, whose rapping the basketball star loved. Shields doesn't have the comparative imagination to think about how Payton's send-ups of white sports writers function in the same arena as the Jewish bad taste both Rodney Dangerfield and Jackie Mason parodied and used as weapons against the stiff and straw WASPs they battle in *Caddyshack* and *Caddyshack II*.

Though Shields cites a number of instances of black people running over or stymieing white people in a social ritual he

interprets variously but never intelligently, our homegrown
Virgil fails to seek a connection between the hostile attitudes
celebrated in popular culture at large and the break with sportsmanship exhibited by many black players. Why would he?
Shields is invested in using black people to uphold his trivial
sense of rebellion, which he exhibits by refusing to obey traffic
laws (whether walking or driving), being rude, and silently
encouraging his daughter to "demolish" Christmas ornaments.
One then wonders why Shields does not examine the ethos of
defilement and destruction that runs through the work of so
many white intellectuals, who seem to feel that defiling and
demolishing form the highway to social heaven: *if you can't fix
it, chip it or break it.* When variations on this do not appear in the
aesthetic forms imposed by men like those nineteenth-century
French intellectuals, artists, and their many descendants on the
high end of culture, it is reduced to the hysterical love of
destruction in the world of rock and roll, where a form of hysteria and fascination with the primitive that appeared in the
1960s has been picked up and extended by rap, which celebrates
brigands in natural blackface. Setting fires on stage and destroy-
ing instruments expresses a frantic rock and roll disrespect for
even the vessels of expression. The slut chic of Madonna is
another way of pushing everything other than one's own
appetites—or pretended appetites—into a heated tub of excrement. Further, in the world of big business, it is not unknown
for white men of position and means to trash hotel suites. This
is even seen among cops. During a 1995 Memorial Day visit to
Washington, D.C., some members of the New York Police Department went berserk at the Hyatt Regency Hotel. Acting like
armed frat boys, they set off fire alarms, ran around in various
states of dress, harassed customers, slid down banisters made
slick by beer, and generally exhibited behavior that would have

shocked their pants off if they hadn't already removed them. From rock to big business to rap to cops. Is anarchic behavior the best response to the weight that civilization imposes on us all? Is this the most we have to offer? Don't ask Shields.

When it comes to ethnic definitions, Shields never wonders what would have happened to Jews (or any other group confused about the strength and the potential of its identity) if they had read the essential tools for social mobility, beyond entertainment and athletics, as insufferable stuff imposed by a culturally taboo national power that should be resisted at every turn. When he does investigate such a question, the results are bracing. In a *New York Times Magazine* article Shields quotes filmmaker John Singleton as saying, "Our children need assets like technology that will lead us into the next century. And they need to learn that it's cool to learn this technology. That it's cool to learn how to use a computer. Enough of basketball. It's about learning how to use this stuff." This reminds the writer of Arthur Ashe, whom he quotes as saying, "We blacks spend too much time on the basketball court and not enough time in the library." Shields lives up to the title of that chapter in *Black Planet,* "Proof of My Own Racism," when he refers to the remarks made by Singleton and Ashe: "These statements make me feel defensive and guilty; they incriminate my romance with the game, but—guess what?—the guilt passes." This is where the book actually becomes a very evil thing.

One in a million kids, literally, will make it to the NBA; far fewer will become rap stars. There is an enormous, tragic fantasy attached to the aspirations of young black men across this nation who are working on their athletic or rapping skills with nothing to back them up, nothing to fall back on, no preparation for gainful employment, no intellectual engagement. Even though Shields hints around the subject or pretends to be looking into it, he does not pore over the ramifications of how successfully far too many black men have been duped—by rap and pop culture in general—into remaining children in a time when being and aspiring to be responsible, educated men is as important as it has ever been for any group at any time in the history of the world.

When one looks at the responses that Booker T. Washington and W.E.B. Du Bois made to the whites who went South during Reconstruction (1865–1877) to educate Negroes, most often with the patience and fire of missionary zeal, we can see the difference between truly taking on the problems of this nation and using those on the lower frequencies for personal amusement of the sort that confirms and reaffirms the minstrelsy that once dominated national images of Negroes. Both Washington and Du Bois, no matter how much they might have disagreed on a number of things, were well aware that education was the best weapon against racism and that being open to education and all that it made possible was the highest form of rebellion against the perception and the limited social access of an ethnic group considered "naturally" stupid and incompetent. What Shields chooses not to know is that until recently Negroes, across the classes, took the position that "Knowledge is freedom; ignorance is slavery." There was no confusion about "white middle-class standards." Racism was endured but not accepted in any form and was yet to be veiled in the term "cultural relativity," which has become part of the condescending language of low expectations. Black people and sympathetic whites looked at things straight on. Basic ignorance and illiteracy were not thought of as fundamental aspects of "black culture." Wrong-headedness and the extreme limitations resulting from not pushing one's intellect were never confused with substantial rebellion. They were discouraged or pitied.

As people should know even without this book, things are far different from what they used to be, in and out of sports. For all the white owners, white coaches, and white referees, Shields and other fans watch an NBA that is now 80 percent black but was 90 percent white forty-five years ago, when color was an unspoken barrier. Descended from people who were considered "black gold" in the cargo holds of slave ships, these black men are now worth far, far more than their collective weight in gold. In fact, one of the pivotal moments in American athletic history had to be when Jerry West, a white man and one of the greatest basketball players of all time, took a plane from California to Florida to offer Shaquille O'Neal a contract with the Los Angeles Lakers that guaranteed him $125 million—an eighth of a *billion* bucks. This means that the Negroes whom Shields and the other fans so admire are multimillionaires, young men who are receiving absurd levels of compensation for playing a boy's game.

These men command absolute respect in and out of the game. They buy new homes for their parents, live in mansions, drive expensive cars, fly first class, wear as much gaudy jewelry as they wish, are sought for endorsements, are loved by children, teenagers, college students, kids in their teens and twenties, adults from their thirties through old age, and good-looking women in the hundreds of thousands, actually the millions (Shields must quiver unstoppably when he dreams of being Gary Payton and imagines the many pretty, pretty ladies of every hue, hair color and hair texture, eye color and eye shape, who would gladly get busy if they had the chance to take it all off, lie back, and pump up against their pick of those "embodiments of the life force").

These men have made their reputations in a set of circumstances separate from those of the world at large. In their universe, aside from the contested fouls called by the referees, we get to see something that seems more and more illusive in American life. This may well account for our national obsession with sports: the games and the players exist on the plane of the objective fact. Sports do not knuckle under to "culturally determined" ideas. This remains true no matter how much is made of the style with which the most gifted and imaginative black athletes play games. It is hardly arguable that Negro athletes, at their best, add a rhythmic style based in what Albert Murray calls "a dance-beat orientation," which is no more, finally, than an Afro-American extension of what that wily Irishman Jim Corbett brought to boxing when he decided that being a moving target was less wearing than standing there toe to toe, pounding and being pounded. Sure, that dance-beat orientation has also worked for Negro ball carriers in football and has made basketball dribbling into a highly coordinated art of syncopation that can be thrilling to watch. But all of those moves don't mean anything unless one remains, however colorfully, individually, and improvisationally, far enough *inside* the rules to earn or assist in the earning of *points*. Otherwise, it's "all flash but no cash."

Those objective facts of high-quality performance, while including the specific techniques of the individual, transcend everything. They also allow great individual performance to be recognized separately from the failure of teammates. Most of all, that inarguable aspect of sports allows statistics and myth to coexist, since the specifics of masterful performance fuel poetic attempts at comprehension of the essentials, clearly the meaning and function of myth. At the end of it all, these black men have proven, in an objective space, that they have worked for what they have, that they are not manufactured by some promotional team, that in their flesh, their sweat, and their abilities, they cannot be dismissed as a version of affirmative action, as just some Negroes who have profited at the expense of more qualified whites. The "even playing field" has worked for them and they have received no favors. Their tolerated lack of sportsmanship is not a reparation for anything; it is proof of the sad fact that our society sees rudeness as a superior version of honesty, especially if the obnoxious one has leaped the hurdle of civilized behavior into "the tub of butter" that is great wealth.

So when we work our way through the false leads and the decoys of false confessions, *Black Planet* is about a Jewish guy who got to the heaven of acceptance by white non-Jews and, finding that world less interesting than he had hoped, uses the Negro to return to the rain forest of the exotic by proxy. That, of course, is something really interesting which updates Norman Mailer's "white Negro" theory to suit our era. But one would have to be a far more interesting and deeply provocative writer than David Shields to bring that stuff to the page.

The Novel
as Blues Suite

Adapted from a talk delivered in Washington, D.C., at the Smithsonian Museum of American History as part of a centennial celebration of Jorge Luis Borges sponsored by the Smithsonian Institution and the Argentine embassy.

1. PRELUDE IN A BLUE CLOAK

In William S. Gibson's *Bruegel*, the writer discusses the great painter's comic masterpiece, *Netherlandish Proverbs*, which is a rich and superior variation on Frans Hogenberg's *The Blue Cloak*. The title refers to a man who literally has had designer wool pulled over his eyes. Gibson points out that the spirit of Bruegel's painting—which sets one hilariously insane action next to another in a realistic setting—is expressed "by Erasmus's Folly as she looks down on earth from the realm of the gods: 'There is no show like it,' she exclaims. 'Good God, what a theatre. How strange are the actions of fools.' Elsewhere Folly tells us that men exhibit so many kinds of folly each day that 'a thousand Democrituses would not be sufficient for laughing at them, and even then there would be work for one more Democritus, to laugh at those who are laughing."" Gibson also reminds us that "Democritus was the ancient philosopher who saw the world only as an object for laughter, in contrast to his companion Heraclitus, who wept at its miseries."

2. THREE FOR THE BLUES

Like Ernest Hemingway and Duke Ellington, Jorge Luis Borges was born in 1899, which made his centennial year one that rose in the fastest company. Beyond sharing a birth year, Borges had aspects of sensibility in common with those two sequoias of achievement, even though his methods, like those of all the very gifted, were his own. Borges and the two North Americans were wanderers, wily and able to improvise solutions to what their aesthetic dreams demanded of them. Each set out seeking something more than the familiarly treated and found things that they had to bring into fighting shape, into championship form. All three understood that one had to get home the best way possible. Each learned that what was out there in the greater world and what was back where one began were both the same and very different, mutually human in the clearest and most magically mysterious sense of the dual meanings so central to art.

The great Ellington was the most miraculous musician produced by jazz and the only one who sustained and enlarged his inventive powers decade after decade, evolving in every direction—as bandleader, arranger, composer, and piano player. Ellington was also something of a fabulist. The tireless bandleader loved to create musical fables in a language that called on just about every kind of American music and whatever caught his fancy from abroad. His talent at maturity was so strong that it was never overwhelmed by a source. Ellington combined the very simple and the very sophisticated, the little riff and the far out harmony, the complex line and the stark rhythm, the simple blues lyric with thick counterpoint. He took from everywhere—the street, the nightclub, the concert hall, the nursery rhyme, you name it. He wrote of places with names like "Blutopia," of ladies in lavender mists, of turquoise clouds, of rude interludes, of activities and conditions such as "the Scrontch" and "the Twitch." At Carnegie Hall in January 1943, with the snow so heavy the musicians had to wade through it carrying their instruments above their heads, Ellington brought together an imposing variety of styles delivered in a mutating form to achieve what he would call, describing his forty-minute *Black, Brown, and Beige*, "a tone parallel to the history of the American Negro." It was almost as if the Melville of *Moby Dick* or the Joyce of *Ulysses* had arrived in jazz and had chosen to move from folk art to fine art, from the plaintive to the joyous, the unconcerned to the reverential in order to expand the aesthetic, intellectual, and emotional scope of his idiom. Later, inspired by characters and situations in Shakespeare, Ellington wrote the suite known as *Such Sweet Thunder*. As musical scholar Bill Dobbins points out, some of the portraits of the Bard's characters are called sonnets because they are fourteen phrases of ten notes a piece, actual iambic pentameter!

The ultimate truth of his art is that in the world of Ellingtonia, there was no above and no below; there was only life presenting the constant challenge of being recast into music, music that could measure up to the vitality of existence or render its pathos or its sensuality or its mystery or its hilarity or its overwhelming wonder. No matter how far he might roam in his subject matter and his compositional devices, Ellington always came back home, which was for him, the blues. For example, the last movement of his *Far East Suite* is entitled "Ad Lib On Nippon" but the work, for all the complexity of the piano introduction, is a blues! Consequently, Ellington, Hemingway, and Borges had much in common. The Midwesterner and the Argentine always knew how to get back to their old stomping grounds as well. In fact, the two writers, as we shall see, both scored classically high marks in works that amounted to their own versions of what Ellington brought off at Carnegie Hall in 1943 but were more specifically rooted in the kind of "moral history" James Joyce sought to illuminate in *Dubliners*. The North American chose the moral history of an era, the South American picked the moral history of the world itself.

Hemingway exerted the greatest influence on the writing of English prose in the twentieth century; his style was laconic, subtle, and marvelously controlled. He was an innovator and came to power at the time that writers like Eliot, Pound, Joyce, and Proust were turning the language and the forms of their disciplines around while those like Picasso and Stravinsky were gaining recognition for having developed new ways of expressing personality through the visual arts and music. Hemingway took a backseat to no one in the transcendent authority he brought to his goals. What he has in common with Ellington and Louis Armstrong is the fact that he was the product of no academy but had spent learning time with the masters of his era.

Ralph Ellison observed that in reading Hemingway material such as the Nick Adams stories during the 1930s he got a feeling that was much closer to that of the blues than anything else he knew of in American fiction. The poetic ache and stoicism at the center of Hemingway's work are what Ellison was referring to and the lyrical means of arriving at it were specific victories the master—nobody's dumb ox—set for himself. Hemingway thought the most important thing a writer of fiction could achieve was that place where prose climbed the wall and ended up in the vast garden of poetry. In *How It Was*, Mary Hemingway, the writer's last wife, quotes him as saying, "Nobody really knows or understands and nobody has ever said the secret. The secret is that it is poetry written into prose and it is the hardest of all things to do." This applied to prose writing of any length.

As a teller of sometimes quite tall tales and a writer who preferred it lean over fatty, Borges would have agreed with what Hemingway said to his wife. It is also fair to say that Borges, like Hemingway the short story writer, was like the jazzmen who made so many three-minute masterpieces in the 78 rpm era, which was the area of documentation where Ellington made scores of his timeless works before the long-playing recording arrived. That poetic ground shared by the two writers extended to the fact that neither one believed in hot houses, where the plants arrived in a space of contrived protection. Hemingway knew that the vast garden of nature is full of insects at merciless war, plants living and dying, Venus flytraps, cactuses presenting themselves as metaphors for realistic paranoia. In his poetic compressions, the beautiful and the tragic were inevitably equal and expressed the vision that the deepest writer was always challenged to acknowledge the essences of hard-earned elevation and certain destruction. There too he shares something with Borges, who was as intrigued by deception as he was by destruction.

3. JUST FOR LAUGHS

Given to devising laughter under the flag of Democritus, Borges was intrigued by deception because he was also a prankster and a joker. Given the epic wit of his creations, one

can imagine him being asked on some afternoon in some cir-
cumscribed situation what exactly he thought about the importance of freedom and his responding that freedom was only so
great in any land as the liberty to tell jokes about *anything*.

That, of course, was not all.

At home on the ground, at ease floating on a blue note into a
ballroom of clouds, familiar with the smell of blood, knowledge-
able of knives and hard death, or attuned to one of those guys
who never has need of anything other than a book and an idea, or
one who has no need of books because the very climate of life—
inside the self and outside in the jeering and lyrical and snarling
world—provides an encyclopedia of dreams and tales too numer-
ous for any library to hold in all their reverberating glory.

For Borges, nothing was more important than bringing to
life what he was thinking about and making the reader a traveler
into another world, side by side with the writer himself. Borges
had no interest in display and obviously knew that the reader is
someone who either takes the writer's word for it or doesn't. He
was less concerned with the reader believing what he had to say
than the reader actually getting from the start to the finish of
the tale, since for Borges the whole point was the experience of
traveling. That is why he followed Edgar Allan Poe's dictum:
keep it brief. That way even the slothful reader might be nabbed
and sentenced to read the last sentence.

Even so, his work is always some sort of voyage into a situation that automatically dispels any relationship to the plain
and simple. That is why poetic command is so important to
his fiction. Poetic compression is a major concern because
Borges believed that the metaphor is all, no matter if it arrived
in an image or a situation or an entire tale or a phoney redress-
ing of historical fact or a parodic dialogue or a hilariously academic review of a classic book as if it were written with

exactly the same words by a later writer! The creator is a maker of metaphors and can be judged by them, just as a society can be assessed by the quality or the lack of quality basic to the metaphors by which it lives.

4. ONE IN THE NORTH, ONE IN THE SOUTH

The first book Borges wrote, *A Universal History of Iniquity*, or *A Universal History of Infamy*—pick your translation—is not a wickedly fanciful collection of short stories published in 1935 but a short novel formed like a suite. *The Universal History* is very losely related to Hemingway's *In Our Time*, which is ordered in a way that the italicized interludes preceding each chapter form, as writer Tom Piazza observes, a corollary to Goya's *Disasters of War*. But those interludes, which are actually very, very short stories, also have a contrapuntal relationship to the other chapter-tales, which are complete in each instance but gain power by their placement and what they do to the overall tone of the book. That overall tone is about pain and death and the inescapable nature of the two.

In Hemingway's world, violence is no more than a heightened version of what is always happening. From his perspective, we are forever consciously or unconsciously preparing for hurt and destruction; we are right in the middle of both; or death—the serial-killing general who is given to protracted strategy and has never lost a campaign—finally gets us into the situation where neither surrender nor resistance changes the outcome. The reaper will be left standing in all his grimness and we will be disappearing or descending or ascending or getting ready to come back around, dependent on what one believes—between heaven and hell, the devil and the deep blue sea, or nothingness and the Hindu vision of reincarnation.

Hemingway, unlike Borges, wasn't concerned with the image of the aftermath of death in the shadow world so susceptible to mythological supposition. Yet the literary pranks that attend the storytelling device of the word "suppose" were at the center of Borges's work because, to the Argentine, the enduring images from our international and collective past are as fundamental to the richest definitions of our humanity as the superbly summoned physical world Hemingway used as ballast for the tragic vision of his work. Hemingway was concerned with maintaining morale when a solitary truth on which the entire world agrees makes itself obvious and ominous in a situation where no god of any sort comes, like the cavalry, to the rescue. He had his mind on the finish line that awaits us all, the one toward which we are running even when we think we are making a getaway. The ever and inevitable open arms of oblivion were his focus. Hemingway created under the flag of Heraclitus. For Borges, however, the telling of a tale with sufficient magic is itself a statement of morale and what all human communities have in common is the presence of stories, either explanatory or speculative, transporting or depressing, fanciful or austere, romantic or hateful, pious or parodic.

Hemingway, no matter how much he developed his power and range, never took form beyond what he achieved with *In Our Time*. He was almost surely influenced by *Dubliners* or *Winesburg, Ohio* or both. But Hemingway did something fresh, paving the way for Borges and for the Faulkner of *Go Down, Moses*, which was, the Mississippi author told the critic Cleanth Brooks, a novel, not a collection. Hemingway wrote in *A Movable Feast* that, during his young days in Paris, "I had been trying with great difficulty to write paragraphs that would be the distillation of what made a novel." This is an extension of Joseph Conrad's idea that every sentence should tell you what is going on, should somehow foreshadow or contain the theme. *In Our Time* is the victory of those distillations. It is not an attempt to avoid the rigors of writing a novel. No. Hemingway is rather boldly asking the question of whether there is another way to write a novel in which one achieves sweep through a dominant character, a Midwestern Odysseus named Nick, and situations that constantly relate to the themes of agony and death.

Though he does not make use of a central character, that is exactly what I believe Borges is doing in his *Universal History*. It is not history in reality because he takes the truth and mangles it with the same freedom those in Hollywood used when making supposedly historical films. Invented events and melodramatic simplicity were assumed the best solutions to achieving good studio profits because those purportedly in the know took the position that the public wouldn't stand for complex depictions of historical figures that didn't live up to the formulaic dimensions of high or low *entertainment*. For one thing, there always had to be a love interest so that women would come to the movies, which meant that a historical figure was given a great love even if he or she never had one. Borges, to be sure, had different intentions. In that first book, the Argentine went toward what he later wrote of in "The Maker," when he identified with Homer, telling us that the epic poet brought *human* distinctions to mythology, making what he had inherited as a Greek equal in its reality to his own life. In his satiric, violent remaking of historical characters and situations, Borges seeks to symbolically connect himself and his readers to thematic tales from just about anywhere on the globe, affirming the proposition of "citizen of the world," as it was once called.

Borges, ever wily, reverses the normal progression of history, which is that it moves from the world of myth, legend, and lie to that of the thoroughly researched fact. Where fact is not available, we get the "educated guess." In the case of Borges, we get what he considered the crux of the matter, the educated lie that is the poetic elevation of the common into the uncommon. Through the untruth of the artist we arrive, as Hemingway observed, at something that feels even truer than the facts. For Borges, these facts are part of a game in which subjects are given every kind of high-handed treatment possible by the writer. Borges also knew that it was important for the writer in the Western Hemisphere to move outside of the exotic narrows. In the interest of that motion, he chose to create a fantastic world for *The Universal History*, one that preceded the single tale of murder set among the hurly-burly thugs and saloon women of Argentina, which concludes the volume from 1935 (though three other pieces were included in the 1954 version).

The one from 1935 is extremely interesting because the varied locales and time periods of the stories reveal the writer as an Odysseus who wanders far and wide before sailing home. In his eight thematic tales of trickery and ruthlessness, Borges starts in the American South, then moves to Australia and from there to Europe, spins a tale of Chinese pirates in Asia, puts us among Manhattan criminals, goes the distance from Manhattan to the cowboy West of Billy the Kid, saunters into Japan, and moves to the Middle East. For the finale, Borges returns to Argentina as a listener, one come home from the world of reinventing his international reading material. The writer himself is the one to whom the concluding tale of foul play is told in the first person, with the author's name arriving in the last sentence of the book. By finishing with a tale of murder in the land of the pampas, he is saying of his homeland that we too in our very own style have produced exactly the kinds of deceptive vermin that the rest of the world has, a mischievous flipping over of the usual position that our people are just as good as anybody else.

Borges seeks to achieve in his *Universal History* a wildcatter's version of what Edmund Wilson described when writing of Jean Michelet's *Introduction to Universal History*:

> The ordinary historian knows what is going to happen in the course of his historical narrative because he knows what has really happened, but Michelet is able to put us back at the upper stages of the stream of time, so that we grope with the people of the past themselves, share their heroic faiths, are dismayed by their unexpected catastrophes, feel, for all our knowledge of after-the-event, that we do not know precisely what is coming.

Borges does this over and over with his cast of bad people. He takes historical fact and makes sure we don't have any idea what is coming up (which puts this work close to Hemingway's decision to wildly move beyond fact and kill off the real and living bullfighter Maera in the italicized paragraph leading into chapter 14 of *In Our Time*). This also makes Borges an improviser, one who uses his material as any jazz musician does who announces a standard song and then, as Louis Armstrong taught us all, drops a note here, adds another there, twisting and turning the original melody, its harmony, and its rhythm until he has achieved something far beyond the facts of the composer's material. As writers, however, Hemingway and Borges are more connected to Ellington the composer, whose arrangements of popular materials amounted to his recomposing them, changing the musical facts, and making us "feel, for all our knowledge . . . that we do not know precisely what is coming."

Borges writes of gunmen, slavers, hustlers, street knuckleheads, Japanese warriors, Chinese pirates, an Islamic Elmer Gantry, peacocking Argentine machos and killers. All are brought together through his sense of the remarkable coinciding with the wings that the imagination gives to even highly unusual facts. Borges wanted to make his tales take to the air, where they would provide mythological entertainments instead of history. As one example, he changed Billy the Kid's real name from William H. Bonney to Bill Harrigan. The legendary Wild West outlaw who was mistakenly thought to be left-handed was transformed into a figure in a left-handed book, one in which the facts were not going to be adhered to; this was a work of the imagination, "based in fact," as they used to say in the movie credits. The *History*, moreover, is most deeply rooted not in historical fiction of any sort, other than the dime novel lies about Davy Crockett and the good and bad guys of the Old West. The work seems to go back further, actually, to the history plays of Shakespeare, or, back even further, to the world of Homer, where gods, fantastic beasts, and human beings share equal positions in the drama of narrative. Part of the point of his *Universal History* is that the most fantastic beast of all is the human being, the one who moves not only by instinct but by codes and laws and religions and untruths and the willingness to break every code other than that of personal satisfaction. Infamy, after all, is the subject. It is essential to the moral history of the species.

Finally, the epic sense of life in our world on this side of the Atlantic was understood well by Jorge Luis Borges. The writer was interested in the phenomenon that is the Western Hemisphere and the bloody ancestral cocktail of greed, religion, and accident that made it so explosive and so innovative. The first paragraph of *The Universal History* anticipates *The Autumn of the Patriarch* in which Garcia Marquez, creating his best novel, uses both *Citizen Kane* and gargantuan sentences that go on for page upon page in order to create a metaphor for what happens once a dictator gives a command that puts all kinds of activity into motion, some comical, some horrific. That initial paragraph of Borges's is also a perfect example of what Albert Murray later called "antagonistic cooperation," the idea being that adversity could, through the luck of circumstances and the nature of a given mixture of people at a given time, result in something even more marvelous in its intensity and reverberations than the brutal tragedy that began the whole business.

That opening paragraph, like "On the Quai at Smyrna," is an overture. For the final version of *In Our Time*, which was published in 1930, Hemingway added those two pages of first-person narration. Along with the horrors of battle, women with dead babies in their arms and women delivering babies behind blankets on rescue ships are discussed in order to intensify the book's formal order by putting birth and death right next to one another. He immediately went to work on that theme in the first chapter-story "Indian Camp," where a birth and a suicide take place at almost the same time. The mistake-ridden craziness and the dehumanizing effects of mortal combat are developed in pieces about World War I and a chilling italicized set of tales about a vigilante murder by Chicago police (who are part of what the headline inventors would give the tabloid moniker of "the war on crime"). We are told of the wrong guys being confidently gunned down and the formal executions in Europe by hanging and firing squad. These too are part of a moral history.

Retreating Greeks intentionally breaking the legs of mules in "On the Quai" shows the cruelty to animals that, for Hemingway, pervades life at large. What happens to those mules foreshadows the book's bullfights, bulls killing picadors' horses in the ring, the deaths of the bulls and the matadors and capturing grasshoppers to be run through by the hooks that will torture the fish Nick catches in the next-to-last episode of the book. By the time Nick is alone with nature and his memories, he has been in American situations where the white man, the Indian, and the Negro functioned together, none free of the weight of servitude, gloom, shock, exploitation, madness, violence, and doom. *In Our Time* concludes with "L'Envoi," a half page in italics that is a parodic and brutal angle on this odyssey of Nick the wanderer. In Hemingway's Thrace, both the Greek king and queen are prisoners, supporters of recent executions but now wondering whether they will be killed. The nationality also takes us back to the beginning, where the legs of the mules were broken by the evacuating Greeks who then dumped the pack animals into the sea.

As if writing a blueprint for what Ellington would bring to his *Black, Brown, and Beige*, the composer's "tonal history of the American Negro," Borges went beyond Hemingway's masterpiece. In order to get at that tonal history, Ellington made clear in the title that his composition, his improvisation in form, would be the history of miscegenation. The many miscegenations that intrigued Ellington were not simple. They arrived as part of social motion. Blood, culture, religion, and sensibility were miscegenated as a people moved up from bondage all the way to the penthouse views of Harlem, rocking and rolling with the punches, the romances, and the revelations along the way. Ellington was a longtime nightlife person, whose middle-class Washington, D.C., background didn't keep him from finding out about the pool halls, the gambling dens, the whorehouses, the all-night jam sessions, the joints where bullets might start flying at any minute and put the young boss of a band under a table, which was where Manhattan bandleader Fletcher Henderson joined him for shelter the time during the middle 1920s, when he brought his top tenor man—Coleman Hawkins—down to Washington to hear a kid who had "something different."

Up north, in the bright lights of the big city that was New York, the Negro stride piano players walked the streets like fabled gladiators, the new dances were invented or arrived immediately, and Ellington eventually got his extended job at the Cotton Club, a room owned and run by gangsters, some of whom were stuffed dead and bullet-ridden in trash cans after they paid a visit to see the floor show, drink the liquor, and have their last party. In that swirl of grace, blood, grease, wealth, perfume, boudoir stink, poverty, and aesthetic grandeur, Ellington came to understand the facts that would later lead him to say that the day that the first unhappy African landed on the shores of what would become the United States was a very happy day for the country to which so much would be contributed by black people.

Borges, perhaps the Ellington of his own continent, laid right into the core of the matter in the complexity of his reading of the history of the Western Hemisphere below the Canadian border. In his overture, no more than an opening but potent paragraph in the first tale, slavery is, again, the ugly truth that made possible the beauty resulting from the Negro influences on North and South America, regardless of how differently those influences developed above and below the equator. Under the heading "The Remote Cause," Borges starts with a sweeping montage set in motion by what he defines as a perverted version of philanthropy. Borges informs us that Charles V's decision— prompted by entreaties from Fray Bartolome de las Casas in 1517—to replace the Indians working in the debilitating mines of the Antilles with Africans initiated what would become a fresh and varied way of living. The result, over the centuries, is "an infinitude of things," good, bad, and ugly. They include—first of all!—the blues of W.C. Handy; the emergence of an incontestably mulatto culture formed of European, African, and Indian influences; voodoo in Haiti and impressive figures such as Toussaint L'Ouverture; the issues that resulted in the high body count of the U.S. Civil War and made Abraham Lincoln into a leader of mythological proportions; films such as King Vidor's *Hallelujah*; legendary military units of dark-skinned Negroes and mulattos; lynchings; murderers; terrible rumbas like "The Peanut Vendor"; awesome dances like the tango; and so on.

No, Borges did not bite his tongue when it came to aesthetically examining the mulatto dimensions of what made the cultural mixtures so open to fruitful exploration. In that regard, Borges even does what I believe is a fascinating and nose-thumbing variation on "The Battler," a masterfully rendered chapter of *In Our Time*. There Nick encounters a boxer reduced to a simpleton by blows to the head. He is taken care of by a dignified former Negro criminal who has to knock him out with a worn leather-covered sap whenever the ex-pug becomes dangerously violent. Given Borges's love of Melville, his variation might also be an oblique take on "Benito Cereno," where Babo, the leader of a slave revolt, deceives the captain of another ship by pretending to be the servant of Cereno, whom he uses like a ventriloquist's dummy while feigning obsequiousness and knowing that no white man would assume that he was actually the one in charge of a ship in apparent chaos. Conversely, had Cereno's ships been transporting European prisoners to a work colony and the barely tempered violence of the prisoners toward his crew been so obvious, the captain would have immediately recognized that a revolt had taken place. Racist condescension held the Africans above suspicion.

In Borges's "The Improbable Impostor Tom Castro," we meet Ebenezer Bogle, an Australian Negro possessed of a genius for the big con. Borges notes of his genius that "some textbooks in anthropology deny the attribute to his race." Bogle, his skull much more a "hive of subtlety" than Babo's, poses as the servant of an ingratiating simpleton whom he meets in Sydney and takes to London after cooking up a very sophisticated plan to pass him off as the long lost son of a high-born lady. Not until the Faulkner of *Go Down, Moses*, would a U.S. writer from the Caucasian side of the tracks imagine a Negro so much faster in the head than the white people surrounding him. Borges, doubting the potential greatness or vileness of no ethnic group and no nationality, was up on another hill from which he could see much farther than what is still a common poverty of imagination in U.S. fiction.

Finally, what makes *The Universal History* so great and Borges such a sequoia is the ambition to live in the entire world through the themes that create an overarching narrative because our humanity is overarching and overreaching. That is what we mean by dreaming and by inspiration. That he was able, as was Hemingway, to create another way of forming a whole, a way of getting to what Ellington might have called a literary blues suite, is another high moment in the definition of a topsy-turvy century. Like Ellington and Hemingway, Borges not only went after life but bagged it, both the visible that is the flesh and the place, and the invisible, which is the spirit and the sensibility. In all, his was a victory for recognition, as all art is. As people of the Western Hemisphere, we are a mix and a mess and given to reinventing something more important than the truth, which is the poetry of our connections, above and below, in the heavens and the sewers, the happy blues, the plaintive blues, and the hilarious blues. When Borges comes on home to Argentina in the first version of his first book, he is exactly like Ellington always returning to the gut bucket of the blues, and Hemingway's Nick, after *In Our Time* has taken him to so many places, going on home to the backwoods fishing country where his heart began to understand how it was made.

The Late, Late Blues: Jazz Modernism

THIS IS AN IMPORTANT BOOK ABOUT JAZZ AND TWENTIETH-century art that arrives late, as do all important books about jazz. The American intellectual community has never been up to the challenge of the music, primarily because it has not been up to the challenge of the Negro, without whom no such music would exist, however many great to excellent to fine to mediocre to terrible white musicians, both Jewish and Christian, have found their identities within the art.

There has always been something about the Negro within the terms of American culture that shut down discussion or inquiry among intellectuals, unless the talk or the writing was condescending or the usually darker American was used as proof of how much bunk there was to all the crowing about the land of the free and the home of the brave. The Negro wearing the barbed wire wreath of American racism around the neck and around or pushed into the genitals was preferred to any other. The idea that the Negro, like everybody else central to the shaping of Americana, could have produced cultural geniuses of all sorts was beyond consideration, especially if we might have to consider how well those geniuses defined the proposition of the nation itself—or, Lord help us, addressed the age.

In a forthcoming book, David Yaffe quotes what Ralph Ellison said in an appearance on a 1965 PBS show about jazz: "One of the most intriguing gaps in American cultural history sprang from the fact that jazz, one of the few American art forms, failed to attract the understanding of our intellectuals. . . the greater job of increasing our understanding is still to be done. A vacuum does exist in our understanding. It is a fact that, for all their important contributions to American culture, no Edmund Wilson, no T.S. Eliot, no Cowley or Kazin has offered us insights into the relationship between this most vital art and the broader aspects of American social life."

This is how it has been even though William Faulkner repeatedly made a case for addressing a difficult national reality and an equally expensive fantasy, both of them resulting from a most complicated interplay. That interplay crossed the lines of color and emerged as an American sensibility formed from opposites and from oppositions so charismatic that the old goddam dialectic achieved synthesis in the symbol of the mulatto or the Creole or the culture raised as much from black as from white, from Europe as from American Indian, something our Mississippi genius made clear as the summer sun in *Go Down, Moses*, where he dropped this glittering bit of "science," as they used to accurately call insight in the streets:

> This Delta. *This land which man has deswamped and denuded and derivered in two generations so that white men can own plantations and commute every night to Memphis and black men can own plantations and ride in Jim Crow cars to Chicago to live in millionaire's mansions on Lakeshore Drive, where white men rent farms and live like niggers*

*and niggers crop on shares and live like animals, where cotton is plant-
ed and grown man-tall in the very cracks of the sidewalks, and usury
and mortgage and bankruptcy and measureless wealth, Chinese and
African and Aryan and Jew, all breed and spawn together until no man
has time to say which one is which nor cares . . .*

Faulkner clearly perceived that stretch, both human and eco-
logical, from the backwoods of our nation to our cities and to
our world of business, realizing something elemental to the
soul, the culture, the economy, and the "many miscegenations"
that haul us up from ethnic provincialism. Yet one could not
expect people like Alfred Kazin, Lionel Trilling, Harold Rosen-
berg, and the rest of the gang called the New York Intellectuals to recognize the importance of the Negro when they had
missed the importance of George Gershwin, Irving Berlin, and
Harold Arlen, even though those guys were Jewish too, and, in
common with said writers, had listened to tales of the old
country and had heard Yiddish spouted around in the home
and on the block. But, in the very deepest sense, they also found
themselves out there in the streets, walking that American walk
and, before long, talking that slang-heavy American talk.

Out there on those streets, Gershwin, Berlin, and Arlen
inhaled Americana and, having good smellers of the sort always
special to the gifted, followed the scent to Harlem—or some
place like Harlem—and heard in the music the soul of the city,
the transcontinental feeling of the blues that so successfully
united the North and the South, which Faulkner summoned
into literature by doing what Duke Ellington had done in *Black,
Brown, and Beige*, the 1943 extended piece and "tone parallel to
the history of the American Negro."

Faulkner was pushing us to perceive an epic that moves from
the Mississippi Delta to the Jim Crow car to the mansion. Not

only did those Jewish musicians come to understand how that blues feeling has elasticity of reference and feeling; they also observed the dance beats that prodded Broadway choreographers in different directions. Such men saw the steps that were invented in Darktown and nationalized by people like Vernon and Irene Castle. They laughed their cakes off at the Negro humor and pantomime that provided so many comedians, from Eddie Cantor to Jerry Lewis to Rodney Dangerfield, with the foundations on which they built their own personalities and reputations, sometimes beginning within the minstrel convention of burnt cork.

Though Susan Sontag recently described herself as "a dancing fool," one cannot imagine any of the other rightfully celebrated Jewish writers and aesthetes going to the floor with anything other than two left feet, or seeing Louis Armstrong and knowing what he represented and who he was—the Negro as world-class master of allusion, reconfiguration, transformation, and improvisation, the essences of jazz. Who could imagine any of them kicking back to some Ellington and absorbing his layered upon layered fascination with the big city and the backwoods, or hearing Coleman Hawkins make the tenor saxophone into a curved instrument through which improvised and highly arpeggiated America opera was blown; or facing the crack of doom and the idealism in the determined lyricism and unprecedented virtuosity of Charlie Parker; or rising in feeling and thought to the challenges laid down by Thelonious Monk as he remade the piano into a metaphor for urban life as he knew it—romantic as soft rain, strong and abrasive as concrete and steel, playful as a bouncing ball, isolated as a single lit cigarette in all of Central Park?

These are truly American creators who could not have become the forces that they were had their work not been preserved and replicated within the terms of technology and the precision engineering that provided the same instruments for aspiring musicians and fans across the nation. Their ancestors had arrived in the holds of slave ships as the black gold of labor cargo; they had been sold as chattel even more times than they had been repeatedly sold out by the nation; they had taken the Christianity taught to them and removed from it an all too pervasive sentimentality so that the tragic essence of the tale of Christ achieved the bottomless pain and the glory of transcendence central to its charisma. Though they had been rebuked and scorned since early in the seventeenth century, theirs too was the world of the recording and the radio broadcast, the printing press and the motion picture, the steel mill and the railroad, the automobile and the cafeteria. They were not only Americans as pure as any others; they were also as modern as anybody else in the twentieth century because part of being modern was responding to life in a modern manner.

Inarguably, the Jewish and Christian intellectuals who missed all of that cannot be separated from the Negroes of the 1920s who considered themselves intellectuals and appreciators of the arts but had, for all of the talk about a "New Negro," no real understanding of what was taking place as those southern Negroes—arrived from New Orleans and wherever else—brought to the big cities visions of jazz that would change the perception of musical possibility with group improvisation and redefine the instruments through fresh techniques bent on rivaling the vocal nuances of Negro blues singers.

That Alfred Appel Jr. is Jewish and in his late sixties and has written a most stirringly brilliant book proves that there is no excuse and there has never been an excuse for missing this phenomenon. In the wake of both Ralph Ellison and Albert Murray, Appel has created what is probably the best book about jazz as an art in the context of *all* modern art. It is a book quite different from those filled with the technical analysis of Gunther Schuller, who towers over all of his competitors, first because he can write and second because he is as capable of describing what makes a great musician wonderful in straight English as he is a frontiersman in his technical discoveries.

Appel cites and addresses a number of writers but makes nothing of either Ellison or Murray, which would seem incredibly egocentric if he had not revealed his peerless self-inflation on page two: "In matters pertaining to race and racial politics, my comparisons and unambiguous assertions should be stimulating if not definitive." Is that so? That Appel goes silent on Ellison's marvelous jazz essays and Murray's invaluable 1976 poetics of jazz, *Stomping the Blues*, puts him solidly in the tradition of white musicians and jazz writers who have used Negro models but remain mum about their sources. In reviewing this book for *The Nation*, David Yaffe charged Appel with rewriting an observation Ellison made about Armstrong, whose artistry the novelist described as Shakespearean in range and complexity. Even while trying to put a lightening Harmon mute to the bell of my own horn, I would have to say that Appel most probably read *Notes of a Hanging Judge* and saw my own "Body and Soul" (1983) in which I compared Negro musicians with Renaissance creators in the visual arts and drew a connection between Picasso and Armstrong. I also recognize in his book things I have been saying in mass media about Fred Astaire for the past decade or so.

No matter: a man who thinks with the originality that he does can be forgiven, especially since *Jazz Modernism* is intended to be experienced as a work of artistic expression at the same time that it is supposed to be an assessment of some central jazz monarchs and empresses of style and invention. It is an autobiography of sensibility, as much about the author as the subject. Appel is asking the reader to see twentieth-century masters of painting and sculpture as he does. He is also asking his readers to hear the music in the way *he* does, accepting his translations of notes and *his* interpretations of vocal *interpretations* of lyrics sometimes too bad to be believed in a nation where too bad to be believed has such a track record that it is an assumed fact (that he also misquotes some of them is also interesting).

Appel has taken the liberties one would expect of an American who has studied the visual arts for many decades, taught literature for forty years, and also was on the scene listening to jazz. In the nightclub world of cigarettes and alcohol, concert circumstances were created because the rooms were too small and the tables too close for dancing. There Appel witnessed some of those signal things about the making of the music and the interplay among the musicians and with the audience that cannot be captured solely in the context of recordings, which remain the greatest available repository of jazz modernism.

What might be considered a unification theory in which the arts of the visible and the invisible are brought together amounts, like the late work of Andre Malraux, to the story of a mind and a heart that never exasperate each other. Like Malraux, Appel is concerned with triumph and the ways in which the private fate becomes public and, through aesthetic form, is relieved of its anonymity while speaking to and for all of those who are anonymous to the world but have in common with the world the troubles and the joys of human existence. Human existence, as we all know, is always accompanied by the mysteries and the clarifications of human passion. In the case of jazz, the Negro's troubles become metaphors for all troubles, just as the specific troubles of Homer's heroes, strapped to their tales by the conventions of the Greek pantheon, become metaphors for the troubles of us all.

Appel puts jazz in a broad context as he discusses recorded performances, advertisements, and the very labels of the recordings that now bring back an era as impressively as the artifacts of older times that preceded precision engineering. Photographs of jazz musicians, buildings, construction workers, dancers, and a number of others are well chosen and well placed, giving the visual side of the book an antiphonal role that both amplifies the text and challenges it. Appel does not miss the symbolic weight falling from the world of cartoons and slapstick as well as the denigrating humor warmed over from the days of the minstrel show. He is sometimes far too fanciful for this reader as he inserts racial meanings or caution in works that seem to me to be *only* recordings. Appel assumes some Armstrong love songs are low-key in order to keep from making white men angry. This seems a crock, particularly since they were recorded around the time Armstrong did his marvelous "Stardust," which is declamatory in its celebration and profoundly romantic in its suggestions, its dropped words, and its added ones, such as "baby low."

What particularly places Appel outside of the arena of most American intellectuals when it comes to Negro aesthetic matters is that he has not fallen for the repulsive limitations of the influential Frankfurt School as expounded by Theodor Adorno and Max Horkheimer, who had contempt for the United States and understood little about how American vernacular art functions or comes into being, and got even less right how the actual dialectic of American aesthetic enlightenment achieves synthesis through the imaginative transformation of the dull, the ugly, and the mindlessly or meretriciously conceived. That imaginative transformation provides us with an object of beauty that, when our culture is lucky, becomes popular enough to speak to and for our nation and the modern world itself. Cognizant of that process, Appel understands America as it is, not what some German somebody thinks it ought to be, especially if that somebody is too far removed from the horror, the beauty, the melodrama, the tragedy, the hopelessness, and the optimism of this nation. America is great because what it actually is so often triumphs over what it should never be; jazz, in the very faith it places on the improviser, is an art ruled by possibility, by the belief in the possible, not the conventions of the impossible.

Adorno and Horkheimer, Ted and Max, failed to understand that the team can function as something more than an extension of the power of the state and the rule of the owners, who produce constricting and debilitating products for the masses. They believed that the conventions of popular entertainment were beyond bending and that creativity was superseded by novelty, the manufactured blip of light on the screen that is sold as a three-dimensional thing. Even a genius like Orson Welles only underlined the power of the cliché to survive his decimation. When Appel writes of Armstrong or Fats Waller or Duke Ellington, he is fully aware of what the jazz artist learned: his arms were *not too short* to box with the commercial god of the cliché or the overstated. Appel understands that for such artists, inspired invention—either second by second on the spot or in the time it took to write either an original piece or a stupendous arrangement—provided an alternative to that expected thing everyone felt already cognizant of in terms of its expressive possibilities.

Armstrong rebukes all of Ted's and Max's theories about the meaninglessness of the individual in popular art and the subjugation of talent in the interest of a culture industry that teaches a public to hunger for an ongoing repetition in which every form uses a similar jargon that deceitfully stands in for expression and artistry. Armstrong refutes such baloney since he is one of those who helped create the true individual in popular art by proving that one's sensibility, however powerfully stylized, can so perfectly take aesthetic command of the present in the act of improvisation that the resulting substance and nuance prove themselves more than vaporous tricks by withstanding the repeated close reexaminations made possible by the recording. This was no small achievement. Played once on the wing, listened to thousands of times the world over, the best jazz fulfills one definition of the masterpiece: a work that cannot be exhausted.

The essence of it is that the improviser proves that the present can be as good as the past: we bring the past into the present to protect us from the abyss of the moment, which we should whenever possible. That is why the concert musician is more like the actor who takes a text from the past and makes it come alive in the present, giving it such vitality—if the actor is great—that those words arrive as if never said before, as if this is the spontaneous expression of emotions felt in the moment. The improviser, on the other hand, is bringing order to the present with material summoned in the present, profoundly turning around most of what we know about creation and destruction. Elsewhere I have pointed out that one of the first things we all learn is that destruction has a much faster velocity than construction. The broken glass, the burned piece of paper, the slaughtered lamb—each is destroyed more quickly than it is created. The best recent example is September 11, 2001. It took a long time to get those towers up, less than an hour for each of them to come crashing down. But what serious improvising posits in the magical world of the aesthetic dimension is the possibility that substantial creation can equal the velocity of destruction. The best jazz recordings break the story and make the case.

Ted and Max had no respect for the Negro or for America; otherwise they, like Appel, could have seen that every successful work of musical art achieved by a Negro was a victory over the assembly line vision of an ethnic group that is what we call the stereotype, the agency at the nub of what Ted and Max were talking about when attacking the culture industry as an instrument of state and business power, a reaffirmation of things as those in power assume they should be. To get right down to it: every time a Negro, boring through the sentimentality and the corny rhythms of a popular ditty, asserted an individuality tangible to perception, a human opening had been blasted through the confines of minstrelsy and stereotypes, one big enough to release fresh air while allowing the audience a hole through which it could peep actual humanity. Such holes transform themselves and always provide the audience with mirrors in which it sees familiar humanity with unfamiliar faces. And since the stereotype is often an offshoot of superstition, another kind of enlightenment, a different kind of scientific revolution arrives as the human being transcends it and makes human recognition the only true form of progress.

Indisputable Dippermouth proof: Armstrong's individuality in public flight inspired white Charles Black to question the Negro's segregated "place" after a 1931 engagement in Austin, Texas. "What was 'the place' of such a man, and of the people from which he sprung?" Black asked himself. Twenty-three years later, in 1954, Black was on Thurgood Marshall's legal team that took down segregation before the Supreme Court.

It would have been too much to ask the New York intellectuals to appreciate the genius of men such as Armstrong and Ellington, for they would have had to think beyond their own conventions. American life would have had to be recognized as something other than a spittoon into which one hawked, following the lead of those revolutionists who celebrate the people for being too crudely pure to fall under the decadent sway of the upper class while hating them for having bad taste or for reminding them too much of their own families, who included few intellectuals among the dregs arriving at Ellis Island after traveling in steerage all the way across the Atlantic. These people came up through the public schools that the Negro legislators of the Reconstruction knew were essential to liberating those forced to exist outside of the world of reading and the world of the mind. Theirs was an aristocracy of readers who were pioneers bringing European visions into a savage land. Intellectual missionaries might have been a better term for them than the New York Intellectuals. One of their watchwords was: *Don't let anyone know that my peasant heritage is as real as my worn and faded library card.*

It is therefore all the more amazing that Appel was able to embrace the high achievements of modern art and writing—and all of the intellectual frontiers that had to be crossed in order to introduce whole new perspectives—while avoiding condescending ideas that rendered American vitality incomprehensible, as well as the context in which it arrived. For this he should be celebrated, however wild his conclusions, however far removed some of his comparisons, and however absurd some of his conclusions. He has done something quite well, for all of that. His eyewitness reports are well told, as when he recalls Stravinsky listening to Charlie Parker at Birdland one night in New York. He recognizes the droll wit and satiric inclinations of Fats Waller though he makes heavy reference to Eudora Welty's "Powerhouse," a story apparently about Waller. It is a terribly square tale about darkies partying the night away in a Mississippi roadhouse. He tells us stories about drummers Big Sid Catlett, Jo Jones, and Buddy Rich that have enormous gravity and atmosphere. All of this arrives in a beautiful hail of reproduced paintings and photographs of sculpture that even those who dislike the book will appreciate.

Blues in More Than One Color: The Films of Quentin Tarantino

Unfortunately, it would take more than a few gems to reverse the damage done. Black audiences' need for assertive black characters in which they saw a reflection of themselves was now paralleled by a new set of stereotypes which merely served to reinforce previously held prejudices. If blacks were no longer slaves, servants or sidekicks then they were pimps, pushers, informers, studs and hot mamas.

BLAXPLOITATION.COM

Silly Caucasian girl likes to play with Samurai swords.

KILL BILL, VOLUME 1

There are two things that Jacques Barzun sees as proof of a society's decadence. The first is a malaise in which

the bizarre and the inept are seen as normal. The
second is a search for faith outside of the culture,
such as those of us who are interested in Islam or
Buddhism. The decadent culture is for and against
nationalism, for and against individualism, for and
against high art, and for and against strict moral and
religious grounding. I think we fit the bill.

WILLIAM CATHERS

I began this voluminous chapter as a letter to the *New York Review of Books* in response to an article by Daniel Mendelsohn published in its December 18, 2003, issue. It was presented as an essay about Quentin Tarantino's *Kill Bill* as well as the screen-writer-director's overall career. What Mendelsohn thought about the film or Tarantino's output in the long, dismissive piece was of no importance to me. What stirred me up was the shallowness of the insights hidden under impressively professional prose. It was another example of how challenging and provocative statements about race, ethnicity, sex, and identity provoke no commentary in otherwise rightly respected publications such as the *New York Review of Books*. Perhaps nowhere else in the world of high-quality periodicals could a writer be allowed to seriously avoid the blaring issues and wish fulfillment that arrive in fantasies now called "appropriation." After all, some response to these subjects should be expected from an essay about a film in which a blonde heroine spends ninety minutes killing off black women, white men, and Asian hordes.

We never learn anything about such stuff from Mendelsohn, who mainly writes about Tarantino's reactions to other films. At this time, we are told, his work is dominated by allusions, quotes, and inside jokes about his own films, which no longer contain characters or dialogue but moving figures on a flat surface. As the one-legged man in an ass-kicking contest, Mendelsohn concludes that "the lack of a sense of intellectual process or judgment that characterizes Tarantino's approach to his movie influences helps explain the ultimately vacant quality of his work, no matter how clever it often is. This is certainly true of *Kill Bill*, but it also goes for the earlier films—the ones 'about people.' When they first came out, I enjoyed the structural cleverness of *Pulp Fiction*, the comfortable plot machinery of *Jackie Brown*, the taut, depraved claustrophobia of *Reservoir Dogs*. And yet when I saw them again recently, I was surprised to find myself bored by all three. In the end, they feel wholly disposable—they're not really about any of the elements they are made up of (crime, guilt, race, violence, even other movies), and it occurs to you that Tarantino doesn't have any ideas about them either. He just thinks they're neat things to build a movie around."

Is anyone in our time making movies that successfully weave those elements together? If so, who? That sort of specific observation about an arena of aesthetic challenge, if the writer addressed it, would challenge him to come up with some ideas of his own. He would have to perceive an artistic objective and clarify for us what levels of examination we in the audience should bring to subjects such as color, ethnicity, crime, and so on. He would have to back up his claim or say that, for now, no one else has brought off the exploration of these themes either. Had he put the John Sayles of *City of Hope* or the Carl Franklin of *One False Move* up against Tarantino and argued for either director's superior examination of the same subjects, it might have been an interesting essay. Of course, it would also have called for some thought and some actual knowledge of attempts to address the epic nature of contemporary life in American film.

But no. Why be bothered with anything like that? Easier to attack Tarantino for his obvious and obscure allusions. That is both lightweight academic posturing and not the point. *All* modern artists, with so, so much material behind them, are in blatant or hidden dialogue with other artists and have their own inside jokes. The point is what Tarantino attempts to tell us about those things that Mendelsohn says his films use as no more than trappings. Whether Tarantino's films or screenplays are good or bad, race and crime and what they reveal to us about our society are *always* what his work is about, which is why he is important. He seems to have no other subjects and, given what the ones he focuses on can provide, there is no need for them.

Tarantino's obsessions and the questions they raise are not encompassed in single-syllable words like "race." As illustrated by Mendelsohn's essay, they remain below the sight lines of those who reside in our shining palaces of intellectual examination, from which stunningly good work on almost *any other* subject is *expected*. But, like Frank Sinatra, our intellectuals remove the line from *Basin Street Blues* that describes it as the place where the light folks and the dark folks meet. If not, the actions of those figures would almost surely be reduced to the complex simplemindedness of statistics and Marxist or Marxist-derived theories. Unfortunately, not one of those gummy sets of statistics or theories tells us much about the ethnic dreams and styles of our culture, which move from one mask to another—like the pea in the shell game—often leaving no more than their gritty marks in the greasy trends of our declining popular arts and fashions.

Today, those dominant masks are white, black, and yellow, and Quentin Tarantino knows that in detail. He understands, as did Ralph Ellison, that black and white Americans are part of each other. Tarantino has updated Ellison's truth because it now has to be expanded if we are to understand what is happening to us. He addresses the latest version of the Western obsession with things Chinese. It first made itself part of the parlor and the horizon in the Western style known as chinoiserie. As compressed in the jacket copy of Dawn Jacobson's *Chinoiserie*, we are told that "the style's origins lie in the extravagant tales of Marco Polo and the merchants' adventures of the seventeenth century. The fantasy of 'Cathay,' the mysterious East, fired the imagination of all Europe with tempting visions of an exotic land. Excitement at the luxury and splendor of eastern imports grew to a fever as Chinese goods entered the salons of the West. In the eighteenth century the French court's devotion to the chinoiserie style led to its adoption throughout Europe, from Palermo to St. Petersburg, while England, equally affected by the passion for all things Chinese, bedecked its houses and gardens with chinoiseries of its own individual kind. Chinoiserie burgeoned throughout the nineteenth century and into the twentieth, emerging as one of Europe's and America's most vigorous and versatile decorative styles." Tarantino knows that in our moment both black and white people have been influenced, as has the world at large, by Asian philosophy, martial arts, and the Japanese economic miracle, which raised our expectations of quality in products such as automobiles, televisions, and audio equipment.

At large in America, much of what people think they know about the identity of any other people arrives not from reading about them but by absorbing true, false, half-true, and fantasy images delivered through television and film. As the critic and thinker Lee Siegel once pointed out to me, violence works as a lingua franca in mass media because there is little need for translation. Good and bad are not hard to express. This is as old a truth as the Punch and Judy shows and the sixteenth-century Italian comedy that preceded them; it is equally true of slapstick and all broad comedy in which violence supplies the narrative with formal exclamation points.

The function of violence in Kung Fu and Samurai movies is that they have remade the act of murder in the popular imagination. Killing has been turned into a higher calling of the sort that every society needs so that its people can protect themselves when the time comes. Once murder becomes an upper-echelon necessity, enemies can be dispatched without the inhibition that results from identifying too closely with the humanity of the other. The Western film once did this, giving the ultimate violent act a noble quality or a quality that was defined by the *purpose* of the one doing the dispatching. The public always wants to know the difference between moral and immoral violence because history, war, life, and crime have taught us all that violence and murder will forever be with us. Tarantino interprets this need—and its implications—so well because he is probably the most brilliant student of American popular culture, good and bad, of his film generation. That is why his films are about loyalty and lying and always ask the question of when and for what reasons the act of murder can be justified. His own mask as the motor-mouth hip nerd of MTV covers over the outstanding insights of an intellectual American artist who can bring the heat as well as the noise and the darkness. His greatest inspiration appears to have been Jean-Luc Godard, and he could easily be the Godard of his moment.

In *True Romance*, Tarantino's first script, the sweep of his cultural interests and the quality of his thought are made clear by the epic vision he brings to the adventures of a couple of young people born and bred on rock and roll, comic books, hamburgers, television, and B movies. This is so true that the hero responds to his girl's suggestion that they leave the States by saying, "I've always wanted to see how television looks in other countries." I do not believe that anyone can understand Tarantino's other work without deeply examining *True Romance*. It provides the foundation on which *Reservoir Dogs, Pulp Fiction, Jackie Brown*, and *Kill Bill* are constructed. Beginning with *True Romance* and looking at them back-to-back reveals Tarantino's themes; then his method of examining certain aspects of American life becomes obvious. Let's see if I know what I'm talking about.

Director Tony Scott says in the DVD package that *True Romance* is a black comedy, and he never experienced so much confidence in a script. But he *did* add a happy ending and he *did* change the time-boggled narrative line that Tarantino prefers to a linear one. Scott, bless him, maintained the weight of the screenplay in essential ways. Tarantino's gifts were not blunted or smothered. Scott expressed himself by providing his version of the images and his style of lighting and cutting, but he always understood that Tarantino achieves most of his authority through the power of his ear. Scott likens his own role to underlining and supporting the words of the script in a way that enhances rather than distracts from the content.

This was a good decision because Tarantino can hear his way across ethnic and class lines, while creating points of general reference that are now common. These common speech idioms prove how porous our society has become, though they might have originated in *supposedly* distant usages heard among Negroes, in the underworld, in the South, among rock and rollers, and in the urban varieties of Jewish praise and insult. Tarantino's command of American speech reveals an epic degree of knowingly drawn ethnic characters—not *types*—which we almost never encounter in our American fiction: working-class whites, "white trash," highly placed Italian American gangsters and their goons,

pimps, drug dealers; cops who speak the slang of law enforcement and the argot of their prisoners; aspiring Jewish film actors
and Jewish film producers.

True Romance starts at the dark and ominous bottom of
Detroit, a motor city staggering under the blows of Japanese
competition in the auto industry. It ends in the high gloss of a
Beverly Hills hotel where a suitcase of cocaine has brought
together the story's central rock and roll couple, the cops, the
Mafiosi, and the Hollywood Jews, all but three of whom die in a
manic gunfight sparked by a violent reaction to a betrayal. There
are drawn guns everywhere and a Babel of shouting. The tension
snaps when the producer who was about to buy the drugs throws
coffee in the face of his assistant, the suave but cowardly Jewish
actor who is wearing a wire and pointedly reveals that he has
betrayed his boss to the police. When the coffee hits the assistant's face, armed cops, armed bodyguards, and loaded-for-bear
Mafiosi move from the chaos of screaming and threatening into
an explosion of carnage as everyone becomes equal through vulnerability. Bullets have no social prejudices. They know nothing
of class or race or religion or romance or hatred or occupation.
Whether or not the targets are intended, hot lead takes down
everyone it hits. This has been known at least since Julius Caesar
was gutted in the Roman Senate and has been a dominant theme
in American film since *Bonnie and Clyde*, the first to put graphic
killing on our cinematic blues plate. Our modern awareness of
this became most evident when John F. Kennedy's brains were
splattered on his wife's pink suit and the decade of American
assassination was announced on that sunny day in Dallas, Texas.

The relationships between fantasy and graphic murder,
between loyalty and betrayal, between sacrifice and selfishness,
drive *True Romance* and make more than a few profound observations along the way. Clarence is the hero who meets his true

love, Alabama, at a triple showing of Kung Fu films starring Sony Chiba, "hands down the best actor in martial arts films today." Clarence is a lonely guy who works in a comic book store. He is obsessed with Elvis Presley, romantic comic book characters, and martial arts. He is a nerd but is not reduced to a robotic source of detailed information, of interests so far removed from the mainstream that his connection to the warmth and weight of common life barely exists. Clarence is a nerd with fire. He loves corny things but is not a square. He has too much heart and too much tenderness and he is too brave. Beyond it all, Clarence is a product of cultural miscegenation and a vehicle Tarantino can use for questioning pop culture.

The questions arise from the need for a code of honor in a generation that believes there is none. Those codes were smashed by the Vietnam War, which remade the image of the American military; by black power, which displaced any high-minded idea of black and white living together; and by the counterculture, which asserted total sexual freedom, took an interest in Eastern religions, and spread drug use across the classes. The idea of valor and honor in military and social situations such as the civil rights movement was replaced by an increasingly bleak blues for America that reached its low point in *Network* (1976). This film told us that characters representing every kind of belief, traditional to radical, could be reduced to empty media stars, just more flesh and blood commodities moving across flat screens and grubbing for ratings. In Ned Beatty's monologue, the mad hero of *Network* is told that the order of big, big money cannot be tampered with, which pushes the plot into total cynicism and gloom. The public destruction of the mad hero establishes the thesis that the American people will submit to an imposed appetite for violent sacrifice in order to avoid recognition of their own helplessness.

The game is much too big and too well worked out for the American citizenry to change. The public will sink in blood to get the feeling of satisfaction or superiority.

In the wake of Watergate, things began to spiral down into the mud. *Anything* became possible. The most powerful man in the world was brought down by two *Washington Post* reporters because of his willingness to use shadow aspects of the government for abusive, private intentions, all of them based in long-term paranoia and resentment. Faith in government faded away, leaving the individual to make up his or her own code from what is most available. Those who try to make their own way in a world of such reductions appear in the paragraphs of Graham Greene and John Le Carre, but are now transposed from the weary and hostile European minor to the loud blue American major.

The pulp-loving couple of *True Romance* emerged in the wake of all this. They are primitives wrapped in the plastic of pop culture, which asserts its power through the obvious and the sentimental. Nuance presents itself through complex situations, not thoughts. What thoughts there are can be reduced to variations on the movie's title. It all comes down to true love, for which all sacrifice is possible—and from which comes all courage, endurance, patience, and faith. In their gaudy but deracinated universe, one can count on nothing other than love. Everything else is bogus. You think that's easy or simple? Try it, the film tells us: living up to true love will break your heart or your face or send you stone cold dead to the market.

Clarence and Alabama live in terms of pulp because neither they nor more educated people—with one exception—ever mention any books that they have read about *anything*. Comic books and magazines are the limits. They sponge up their attitudes from mass media, but their reactions are not melodramatic because the circumstances are just too goddam violent.

Violence grounds everything, and the couple learns about the difference between seeing an Asian actor die in a choreographed film scene and actually killing another person, no matter how justified it may seem. There is also a difference between promising to stand up to whatever is demanded in the name of love and actually facing demands as dangerous as any in the gory fairy-tale world of action movies.

These differences are revealed in five violent sequences: (1) a drug murder committed by the pimp Drexl that establishes him as a human dragon of our time, (2) a confrontation that involves Clarence, (3) the torture and interrogation of Clarence's father, (4) the torture of Alabama, and (5) what could be called "The Gang's All Here," as a suitcase of cocaine draws everyone together, creating the connections between the known and the unknown that come of our drug culture.

I. IN THE HALL OF THE DRAGON KING

Tarantino becomes especially insightful when he questions the nature of the fantasy chosen as a rejoinder to the cardboard morality and high-minded rules no one adheres to anymore. This is made clear when Clarence faces Drexl, who murdered two men in a previous scene while rap videos blasted from an elevated television on the wall in a motel room. Drexl is the real thing often celebrated in rap—a drug dealer and whore runner. But is he real? Not by a long one. Drexl is actually a dreadlocked white man who imagines himself to be a Negro and wears the African kitsch fashion compatible with the part he has chosen for himself. Clarence dresses like Elvis Presley, the spiritual king of his personal world, perhaps the oldest *human* reference in the film, the one who served as a model for acceptable bad taste, the national and commercial elevation of teenage emotion, and the reduction of sophistication we call rock and roll, which values overstated romantic sentiment and hysteria above all. Clarence drives to meet Drexl in a purple Cadillac that has fake leopard skin on its dashboard. Drexl greets him wearing a necklace with plastic jungle motifs and a leopard robe. The bad taste of cheap animal patterns creates a flimsy bond.

The junior white rock and roll hero intends to kill his would-be black adversary. The ghost of Elvis tells him to do this when Clarence becomes enraged at the information that Alabama—whom he fell in love with and married after they spent one night together—recently had a pimp. When asked if he is black, Alabama answers that "he thinks he is" and goes on to say that Drexl claims an Apache mother but she doubts it. Elvis explains to Clarence that he is not limited to *dreaming* about killing Drexl, he can do it. If every pimp in the world got two bullets in the back of the head, the police would have a party. All Clarence has to do is make sure he's not there with a smoking gun in his hand when the law arrives. What Clarence says to Alabama before he goes to see Drexl, ostensibly to get her clothes, masks his intentions: "I need to do this. I want you to know that you can always count on me to protect you."

Odd as it might seem, Tarantino is raising the issue of wholesomeness. Plucking his very own blues guitar, he has a very unconventional idea about things as they are. We are apparently being told that now might be the time for white men—or *all* men—to kill off their fantasies about being the worst kind of black man imaginable. That model is as rotten as anything else, which is why *The Mack,* from 1973, is playing in the background as Clarence and Drexl argue before going to blows. In the pimp's lair the movie is playing on an elevated television, just like the one in the motel where Drexl coldly murdered for the cocaine. This gesture connects the worst of blaxploitation to the worst of rap, something no other screenwriter realized at that point.

As expressions of the most pernicious side of black popular culture, blaxploitation and rap are the declared enemies of love and romance. *The Mack* is an example of the blaxploitation films that celebrated pimps for being pure rebels who made their own rules, choosing to live outside of the white man's laws and beyond his versions of good and evil. Their basic sense of glamour was so boldly overstated that one was supposed to look with awe at the brightly dyed fur hats and coats, the absurd, king-size jewelry, and the rest of the expensive buffoon outfits.

Blaxploitation films told us that we should take the pimp's code seriously, which was pure, unrestrained worship of material acquisition founded in the cunning manipulation of masochistic women. If life had an alpha and an omega, they were fused in money, which the *chumps* never picked up on because they were too busy *falling in love* and *working* for a living. Pimps did *not* work, they hustled. The only ones who truly understood the facts of life were the players, the gentlemen of leisure, the runners of bitches and the manhandlers of hos. The pimp had a heart as cold as a meat locker and pockets as deep as the Grand Canyon. He was free of all sentimentality. That was why the white man was always trying to fuck with him. That cracker wasn't nothing but a jealous lame. Hell, he wished *he* could pimp, but he wasn't nothing but a flat-backed lame; papa redneck didn't have *no* game.

Tarantino takes off the rose-colored pop glasses. His perspective carries some harsh facts about the national life. There is no vitality to the rebel if he is merely a narcissistic criminal whose only power arrives through lying, cheating, and savage disregard for the humanity of others. Pure crime has no relation to rebellion of the sort that improved American life by working against the limitations and prejudices of society. Clarence learns from Alabama that her pimp is a violent, amoral exploiter who slapped one of her friends around and kicked her in the stomach. As a drug dealer, this ersatz rebel lives at the center of the murderous violence and humiliation that peak in the ritual homicides and consequences of drug dealing and drug use.

Drexl is no bad boy dandy with plenty of bark but no bite. He is a nightmare with his badly scarred face, gold teeth, and Afro getup. At their meeting, he calls Clarence a "white boy" and even tells him, after he has been subdued in a bloody fistfight, "This is not white boy day!" In Paul Shrader's *Patty Hearst* (1988), the character of Bill Harris, lightly corked and Afrowigged, talks into the mirror as he practices a black street accent and verbalizes the left-wing radical Caucasian's absorption of black "revolutionary" contempt for "white boys." This was an all-encompassing term for the pampered, the soft, the middleclass, the intellectual, the frightened, the immasculine—the people who can talk but can't act.

Clarence is so terribly beaten by Drexl and his fat black henchman that the audience is supposed to feel affirmed when the junior Elvis emasculates the pimp by firing bullets from a hidden pistol into his groin before killing him and his greasy sidekick. Our morality is strained by this rough justice even though Drexl presumably would have murdered Clarence and put Alabama back on the street, selling her white trash cheeks, if given the chance. Alabama, however, sees the action as what it is: "so romantic." This is what happens when the world has fallen down and is crushed beneath complicated reactions to the pressure of living; there is nothing left but the basics, which now arrive in pulp versions. But they can achieve a horrifying poetic power through *action*, which provides the crucible out of which the recast foundations of civilization are drawn, *piping hot*: true love, the avenging of a lady's honor, the killing of a dragon in his cave.

II. The Moors *Are* Niggers

The second violent scene involves Clarence's father and a Mafia don, played respectively and exquisitely by Dennis Hopper and Christopher Walken. When leaving Drexl's place, bloodied and enraged, Clarence took the suitcase full of cocaine, thinking it contained Alabama's clothes. Now the pimp's "business associates," beautifully dressed Sicilians, are out to pull the narcotics back into their structure of amoral, unperturbed corruption. There is no limit to what they are willing to do. Clarence's father, once a cop, is now a night watchman who has not heard from him in about three years. When Clarence asks his father to find out from his friends on the police force what they know about Drexl's murder, he is initially rebuffed. He reminds his father that he—unlike *everybody else* in their family—has *never* attacked him for being a drunk and not doing anything for his son. This is the first time he has ever asked him for a favor. The father finds out that the police know nothing. The ghost of Elvis seems to have been right. After Clarence and Alabama leave for California, the father has a chance to face the grim fact that he must express his own version of true love by sacrificing his life for his son.

In one of the finest scenes in American cinema, the father realizes under torture that he will reveal Clarence's whereabouts and decides to provoke the Mafia man into killing him before he spills the beans. It is a fresh version of Hemingway's "grace under pressure." How Tarantino arrived at it is a signal example of his creativity and the breadth of the social world from which he draws his ideas. In the *True Romance* DVD package, Tarantino tells us that he got the idea for the scene from one of his mother's black friends, Big Don. Big D often told him that the Moors, on conquering Sicily, permanently altered the bloodline by impregnating so many women that Sicilians were now distinguished by dark hair and dark skin. Choosing to insert that bit of history into a conversation between two white men was a singularly inspired decision. The upending of the don's smugness is completely believable.

Again we are made witness to Tarantino's fascination with miscegenation of every kind. In this instance, not only are the well-groomed, well-dressed gangsters different from what they appear to be, but they are also different from what they assume they are. That is why the words "Sicilians were spawned by niggers" have such a purposeful sting—especially when the father says that he learned it from studying history and confidently asks of the don, who claims to be an expert on the facial expressions of liars, "Am I lying?" Wait. Perhaps we are talking about the cat clawing its way out of the bag. Could it be that these proud men know or suspect that they, lacking blonde hair and blue eyes, are not the "pure" Italians others think they are? After all, northern Italians often refer to Sicilians as "Africans." Could they, as certain very light-skinned Negroes have always done, be *passing for white?* At this point, all Mafia films since *The Godfather*—the first to portray high-level Italian gangsters glibly spouting racist contempt toward black people—are given a very, very different historical subtext.

Another point that Tarantino makes is central to American social thought: we don't always know exactly what we're looking at. This has been true of art since the time Odysseus disguised himself as a beggar in order to get the drop on Penelope's suitors, all of whom he slaughtered. But it means something else in this nation, where freedom of movement and open access to the surfaces of respectability are available to anyone who can foot the bill. That fluidity is shown when the Sicilian don does not literally reveal his barbaric heart on sight as Drexl does, though the two are separated only by degrees of criminal power and appearance. While Drexl uses black street argot, the don speaks of himself in Christian imagery, almost loftily, "I'm the Antichrist. You get me in a vendetta kind of mood, you will tell the angels in heaven that you had never seen pure evil so singularly personified as you did in the face of the man who killed you." Clearly nothing Drexl would do exceeds the don's willingness to resort to intimidation, torture, and murder. So the pimp and the don represent the two heads of crime that bedevil America, one obvious, the other far from obvious. (Another difference is that, far from being insulted to the point of murder, Drexl would have been elated if he had been told that his family line had been "spawned by niggers.")

In our fundamental literature, Hawthorne told us this, as did Melville and Twain. On the silver screen D. W. Griffith made it clear in *Intolerance*, as did Mervyn LeRoy in *Little Caesar* when Rico meets "Big Boy," the clean-cut businessman behind the rackets. This was old news by the time it was explicitly restated in *Godfather II*, where we saw that appearances had nothing to do with essences—nor did elected political station or the brinkmanship of international business, from telephone companies to the growers and sellers of fruit and sugar. Corruption missed no corner of society or commerce; only those with insufficiently developed noses failed to catch the odor of rot as it curled its way into the air of many rooms.

III. LIKE A NINJA

The third confrontation takes place in Los Angles after Clarence and Alabama drive there to set up a dope deal with a tough Jewish producer through his weak Jewish assistant. After meeting at an amusement park, where the supercilious assistant vomits following a ride on a roller coaster, Alabama asks Clarence if she played her part "like a ninja" at the meeting. He tells her that she did, unaware that the blonde girl from Tallahassee who claims to be "a really good person," not "damaged goods" or "what they call Florida white trash," will have her ninja mettle tested one more time in an excruciating way.

A comical pothead lives with Clarence's actor friend, who puts him in contact with the producer's assistant. The pothead, who never knows what is going on, reveals the name of the motel where Clarence and Alabama are living when he is queried by a member of the Mafia team sent west to bring their narcotics back to Detroit. The goon is there when Alabama enters the motel room alone. He beats her terribly as she tries to hold him at bay until Clarence returns to save her.

The beating has nothing to do with Mendelsohn's offhand interpretation: "When the hit man played by James Gandolfini in *True Romance* methodically beats a gamine young woman, prior to his planned shooting of her, and her increasingly bruised and bloody face keeps filling the screen, we know that he's just doing his job." This is would-be hip academic thinking at its worst. Just doing his job? His job is *torture* and *murder*, and the graphic depiction of that job is meant to let the audience in on the difference between the smooth, mild-mannered speech of the gangster and how far removed his self-presentation is from the base methods he uses to get information. Each time Alabama's battering comes on the screen, we understand with greater depth what a monster in action this man is. The uncomfortable images reveal just what a real gangster *is*. The job that he does is central to what forever threatens civilization. But we *have* heard Mendelsohn's explanation before, quite firmly and with a chill on top: it was used at Nuremberg. The second point of the scene is that Alabama experiences a merciless rite of passage which proves her true love for Clarence and asks her to become a homemade ninja.

We expect Clarence to burst in at any moment and save her. But he does not. Something more realistic takes place as she begins furiously improvising in the face of a deadly situation. This is a deeply rooted American cinematic idea about victory over the bad guy or the horror film monster. Filmmakers have so frequently celebrated the ability to handle danger with improvisation that we are hardly surprised when an improvising character dramatically shifts power relationships in an uncontrived fashion.

Alabama takes her lumps until the goon throws her into the bathtub after she drives a corkscrew through his foot. Rising from the shattered glass of the shower doors, Alabama distracts the gangster by laughing at him and observing that he looks ridiculous because his head is bloody from a plaster Elvis bust she has broken over it. The goon looks in the bathroom mirror. She rubs burning perfume in his face and hair then pounds him on his back with the marble top of the toilet. He draws his gun. Then Alabama sets him afire using a spray can and a flame. Like all impressive American improvisation, it comes out of nowhere but works due to the speed and the accuracy this character shows as she thinks in motion. It also makes American the ninja code of using any kind of weapon: a corkscrew, an Elvis bust, perfume, the top of a toilet, a spray can, and cigarette lighter. By the time she has him down on the carpet outside of the bathroom, Alabama empties the gangster's shotgun into his body and begins screaming with sheer rage and hysteria. She has lived up to her dream of being a ninja for Clarence, but the price has not been small.

This graphic confrontation affirmed a new direction that broke with the progressively violent treatment of women in American film. The democratic, harmless pie in the face that occurred over and over in silent film comedies became the insulting *Public Enemy* grapefruit James Cagney pushed into the mug of his irritating gun moll in 1931. This was followed by many slaps. The level of violence was more ominous by 1953, when Gloria Grahame was disfigured by Lee Marvin with a pot of hot coffee in the film noir *The Big Heat*. The stabbing of Janet Leigh made *Psycho* (1960) a dividing line between the violence of the past and the violence of the future. Nothing since the Coke bottle that breaks the jaw of the gangster's girlfriend in *The Long Goodbye* (1973) has been as frightening, even the manipulative formula genres of slice-and-dice films with nuts loose from the looney bin or nearly invincible white-masked slashers. None of those women (outside of the horror films) fought back well enough to merit some sort of physical respect.

In having Alabama save herself, Tarantino recognizes how frontier females had changed in the city, where white women's strength was taken from them in favor of gentility or urbanization. In films they became *all mouth*, partly because so many of the great parts were written by Jewish men and women. Those Jews—unlike the rough and ready ones who inhabited the streets from which so many of them came—lived in a Hollywood world where one *could* be all mouth or say all kinds of terrible things and *never* have to think about taking an ass whipping. The wisecracking films in which characters had nothing to back themselves up with other than their voices were the forerunners of the Woody Allen films in which physical action, outside of some light kissing and petting, is reduced to anxiously walking up the street and is made fun of at every opportunity. Even the *idea* of physical action and virtue remains outside of the frame.

But that is not how contemporary white women live, nor is it responsive to their collective fear of bodily harm. Newspapers, radio, and television news make them well aware that physical action can mean the difference between being beaten and mugged or raped or, in the most insidious depths of assault, murdered by a serial killer as handsome as the sweet-faced boy next door. These are rare instances, of course, but they are out there and everybody is well aware of them.

Alabama is not buffed up nor is she a master of martial arts. Her specialty is one-handed cartwheels. The audience witnesses nothing in her defensive actions that are phony, magical, or beyond the realm of belief. She is a small woman whose willingness to endure, fight, and think at emergency speed is what matters. She is the updated frontier woman who has been central to the images of women in movies over the past thirty-five years. Tarantino has not missed this. In a rugged time, we are observing the reclamation of an identity that goes deep into the history of the nineteenth-century white woman. The white woman did not have the rigors of slavery to toughen up her femininity, as we are told the black woman did, but she took part in the winning of the West, and that very winning called for a woman who had no serious precedents in Western society since the mythic goddesses of Mount Olympus. Consequently we cannot forget the basic aspects of the image of the white woman in Hollywood westerns: she could be hardheaded and independent or she could be someone a guy could depend on to help build a home out of the wilderness; she could nurture her family with tenderness and attention while not softening up, and use her firearms to fight off brutal white or Mexican desperadoes or wild Indians. Sometimes she couldn't be forced out of her buckskin with anything less than a crowbar, but she could usually put on a dress, let her hair down or sweep it up, and become a beautiful cactus rose when the romantic lamp was lit. That was the all-American girl of the western: ready for everything from a shoot-out to a romance. Through his artistry, Tarantino allowed Alabama—terribly battered but not bowed—to leap into that pantheon through a tight, wounding hoop of knives.

IV. THE MAGNETIC SUITCASE

The suitcase that contains $500,000 worth of uncut cocaine draws together all of the guns that create the cataclysmic final scene in *True Romance*. This is how our world presently works: drugs have replaced sex as the magnet that disrupts the distances between high, middle, and low. As Jelly Roll Morton told us, one hundred years ago the common man and the upper-class man could be found standing close enough to exchange lice at the bar of a New Orleans sporting house. Since then drugs and the desire for the sensation they provide have seeped into the entire social fabric. We saw the reflection of this in the montage of still images in *Superfly* (1972); by then cocaine consumption had moved from hard hat work sites to the expensive apartments of upper-class guys and gals, stopping along the way for anyone who had a taste for happy dust and the ducats to cop a blow.

Superfly worked in polluting conjunction with *The Mack*. Its hero was not a pimp but a glamorized drug dealer who popularized the coke spoon around the neck as a fashion accessory among teenagers in the blue-collar black community. We cannot know how many young men went into the world of drug sales because of it. This is not a question of censorship; such influences raise the issue of how poorly metaphors communicate to audiences who rarely read, no matter their color, religion, or ethnic background. As we learn from the history of the theater, unsophisticated audience members took to the stage to save the endangered heroine, not recognizing the distance between presentation and reality. I doubt there is a more unsophisticated audience than American teenagers. Our social tale since the middle 1950s has clearly proven that.

Part of the lasting power of *True Romance* is that it creates a magnetic couple on the run but has little relationship to films that elevate criminals. It is impossible for the audience—even one composed solely of teenagers—to side with the bad guys, however well written and real they might seem. The monstrous quality of its pimps and gangsters cannot be mistaken for anything other than what it is. At the same time, the film creates an ambivalence toward Clarence's contradictory motives. Elvis junior sees a big score in selling the cocaine, but his decision to keep the suitcase brings about his father's death. When his father was confronted with gangsters and the fix that his son had put him in, he could have told the gangsters where his son and his new wife were headed. But he had to know that he would have been murdered anyway. Clarence's greed brought about the situation, but the father's choice was the same: he fast-forwards his own murder to protect his son, even though that wild, naive boy had betrayed him by not saying anything about the suitcase. Had he known, the father might have disappeared along with Clarence and Alabama, given that he was an ex-cop who had to know how the Mafia reacted when its back was up.

Even so, we forgive Clarence his heavy-handed mistakes, tough-guy poses, and self-destructive guile because of his inexperience; we let him off for his innocence. We particularly appreciate his courage and the ever ready confidence that he can dredge up from somewhere inside himself when necessary. We give him what amounts to the most slack, finally, for something essential to any penetrating romantic tale: the great tenderness he feels for Alabama that comes to the fore in almost every situation. That tenderness might be inspired by examples from comic books or bad love songs or the rest of the adolescent mush that weighs down pop culture, yet the sources are of no significance. Clarence brings the grace of emotional authenticity, as do so many who begin in the lower depths, among the insufficiently realized ideas and cultural forms of our society, down there where the plaster of paris statuette is ever available to stand in for the real thing. The romantic hero's indispensable tenderness rises through all of Clarence's inarticulate or inadequate descriptions. This is *always* the human miracle and it is the quality that the female protagonist *always* responds to in her guy. He knows how to go easy when too much pressure won't tell the truth. He proves that truly delicate feeling for a woman doesn't only challenge the province of worship; it can transform a man into the best version of himself. That is Clarence's strength, but his naive, self-destructive guile sets the stage for bloody horror.

With the exception of Clarence killing Drexl, every act of violence is connected to the suitcase of drugs. Though the world Clarence and Alabama travel through is big and contains a marvelous set of characters, it still exists within the small range of Clarence's mind. It starts at the bottom of criminal Detroit and moves up to the top, which is rubbing shoulders with a filmmaker, a producer highly esteemed among dreamers like Clarence and the hard-nosed cops alike. Clarence's fantasy dialogues with Elvis are one thing; his actual meeting with a real producer is something else, for there is no greater communicator than the feature film, no entity capable of pulling together so many people from so many backgrounds. Everyone knows that Lenin is outdated. Religion is not the opiate of the masses in our time; the twin heads of popular entertainment are, with film edging the popularity of teenage emotion expressed through the howl of rock and the hostile, chanted doggerel of rap. Clarence speaks to Elvis only in bathrooms. He charms, bullshits, and cons the producer in a suite, putting in the hook by first complimenting him for his work. Clarence says that he agrees with men he knew who fought in Vietnam: the producer's *Coming Home in a Body Bag* was the best of them all.

In the Beverly Hills hotel, so far away from the Detroit motel where Drexl murdered two men for the suitcase, the Jewish producer knows he is stepping into a business where gun battles can be as savage as any in a small war. The producer wants no trouble but has two well-armed bodyguards in his room with him. He believes he has everything covered. What he does not know is that his assistant, the one who brought Clarence and Alabama to him, is wearing a wire and that the cops are next door waiting to make an arrest once they hear the producer utter the magic words of intention to purchase the drugs on the spot. The assistant was pulled over in the producer's convertible while speeding along and laughing uproariously. We discover his joy was sparked by how well a bimbo was performing fellatio. He blamed her for making him drive too fast. Refusing to hide the dope, she broke a big plastic bag of cocaine in his face just before a cop walked to the driver's side of the car. When threatened with prison time by the cops and facing an opportunity to learn to be very sensitive to a woman's needs behind bars (because he would be taught how it feels to be one), the assistant agreed to betray his boss and save himself.

The producer's films have grossed more than $1 billion. The cops talk about what "a great fucking movie" *Coming Home in a Body Bag* was as they sit in their superior's office and plan to bring the producer down. Here is the irony and the corruption that drugs have brought into the culture. The producer does *not* need the money that he could make from selling drugs to get back his investment. Respect and success are already his in *very* big numbers. He doesn't usually spend $200,000, even if it brings him half a million bucks worth of drugs. It's not his business. But he can't resist the *bargain*. He just can't. Angry at the costs of his new film, he is convinced that someone is robbing him, which puts him in the mood to recoup some losses. The offer is too, too tempting.

The cops are not prepared for how well armed the producer's bodyguards are when they burst into the room. The Mafiosi, who have been told where everyone is by the actor's pothead roommate, are unaware that there are bodyguards and police in the suite when they kick the other door in. So now we have the rock and roll couple, the aspiring actor, the producer's assistant, the producer, the cops, and the gangsters, all of whom would probably never have encountered one another had not cocaine brought them to the same place at the same time. The slaughter that ensues is the exact opposite of the democratic ideals we hear in jazz or see in sports and the military, where the worth of the individual trumps origins or ethnicity or religion or class. It is the democracy of greed, wrongdoing, bad intentions, betrayal, and law enforcement.

True Romance fulfills a cycle that began in the 1960s and reached its apotheosis by the end of the 1970s. *Bonnie and Clyde* and *The Wild Bunch* had remade the tale of the outlaw couple and the western; *The Godfather* and *Godfather II* told us a shadow government of gangsters and corporations ruled the world; *The Conversation*, *The Parallex View*, and *Three Days of the Condor* asserted that the great enemy of American freedom did its amoral work from within law enforcement and the espionage agencies created by the federal government; *Taxi Driver* took the position that the lone man willing to stand up to moral corruption might be psychotic; and *Coming Home* said that a warmonger could lose his wife, both emotionally and sexually, to a paraplegic. The variations have been many. Eventually the presidency, the government, the military, the FBI, the CIA, and the Mafia were depicted as one protean snake, which meant that America and American patriotism were seen as sucker grooves by the time Tarantino's work first filled the silver screen. Shadow forces dominated all, hiding behind the tattered flag and the yellowed billboards of Mom, Dad, Sis, and Bud. The song from the *Mad Max* series, sung in an exaggerated rock style by Tina Turner says it all, "We Don't Need Another Hero." In such a world, *True Romance* takes a simple stand as old as film itself: when it comes down to the nub of all possibilities, love, courage, and loyalty are the only things that can bring the species through.

In *Reservoir Dogs,* we get one side of Tarantino's style full out. Its premises are simple. The robbery of a jewelry store turns into a brutal mess because the robbers are infiltrated by an undercover cop. Overlapping sequences tell us who's who. Information is controlled by the writer and the director, arriving not in order but in a way that creates tension and release free of linear storytelling. This style allows the writer and the director to take complete control of the time, which is one of the essences of novel writing. The element of surprise, of not knowing what is going to happen next, is made stronger because the audience doesn't know which previous sequence it will be taken into—the near past or the present, both of which are juggled until all time becomes coterminous, visceral, or humorous.

The pop culture banter, which has no function but to establish character, takes off immediately. In a while we discover who the informer is and our sympathy, which has already been directed toward the badly wounded robber, comes all the way up to the top when we discover that he is the undercover cop.

Like Clarence in *True Romance*, the cop is responsible for people dying. He worked his way into the nest of robbers and informed the police of where and when the robbery would take place. In so doing he inadvertently brings about the deaths of those who were shot by one of the robbers for pressing an alarm, thinking they were responsible for the sudden appearance of police officers. To complicate matters even more, a woman was shot through the head by the undercover cop after she wounded him in the stomach as he and another robber tried to jack her car while fleeing the botched robbery. We don't learn until halfway through the film which of the robbers is the cop, and when we do, Tarantino expands his vision to include black and white alliances that will be given variations, for bad or for good, in *Pulp Fiction* and *Jackie Brown*. First we see him surprising us with symbols of race.

By now we understand that symbols are the gateways to fantasy and through them we can understand how ethnic groups are seen. In almost every situation involving a black man in Ernest Hemingway's fiction, he is either noble or troublesome or deserving of a pummeling or a defeat at arm wrestling. No one understands these contradictions better than Tarantino. In *Reservoir Dogs*, he moves beyond Scorcese, who was the first to give us racist conversations or commentary about black people from your average white criminal, not those unmasked gargoyles at the top of Coppola's Mafia cathedral.

There has been much written about this first film directed by Tarantino, but nothing has been made of the conversation among the robbers that focuses on attitudes toward black women (e.g., blaxploitation goddess Pam Grier). It serves up the observation that a number of those black men who "treat their women like shit" might well chill out when they get home with those women and close the door. No one has observed that one of Tarantino's themes (which will be furthered in *Jackie Brown*) is that beyond all the bullshit, there can be a relationship between black and white people that works against the people who are menaces to society.

Yes, menaces to society. Building on *True Romance,* Tarantino again makes brutally plain what gangsters, in their practiced willingness to kill and torture, *are.* If there is anything to admire about these men, it is on the ironically snowy surface; the inside is as dark as a coal mine at midnight. They are not just men who tell gutter jokes and horse around, or men who show the limited loyalties characteristic of the criminal world in which "me, myself, and I" remains the central anthem. These men are robbers who become killers whenever they deem it necessary.

The numbing violence is only superficially attached to academic ideas. We are learning or are being reminded of the same things that forensic scientists address as they analyze professional or amateur killings. This is what the relaxation of censorship made possible for those like Coppola and Scorcese whose precedents of blood and gore had artistic ends in mind, and those artistic ends are what separate them and Tarantino from the cinematic exploiters whose violence is not part of the drama but *is itself the drama,* primarily because their stories tell us nothing and are not meant to tell us anything. Such violence is a substitute for *the intensification of character that is always the goal of the artist.* The artist almost never uses murder or torture for the kinds of narrative exclamation points that characterize slapstick comedy. Yes, death and murder can be comical now and then, but they are not usually laughing matters. That is why almost all the jokes in *Reservoir Dogs* catch in the throat of the audience when it realizes what terrible men it is watching.

The theme of black and white allying against such amoral menaces to society is laid out when we are shown that the undercover cop was tutored in how to do his job by a veteran black cop who not only supplies him with a story he should tell the criminals but directs him in order to make sure that he delivers it correctly. For the first time in a heist film, the black veteran teaches the undercover cop how to talk authentically among white criminals who have no trouble using racist epithets or criticizing one another when they either "talk like niggers" or "act like niggers." But it is not that simple. Tarantino is too fast for that. Superficially these men might seem no more than crude racists, but they do not moon over blondes; they admire black women, see them as sex symbols, follow them in blaxploitation films and television shows. They even take the position that there is only so much a black woman will take from a man before she "fucks him up." They also tell tales about black women they *know* in order to point out how a woman can handle an abusive guy. Perhaps most surprising is the remorse and anger two of them feel after the robbery when they reflect on how a young black woman was cut down by the psychopath among them the moment the heist went haywire.

As criminals, they live in a physical universe where cleverness and nerve often stand in for intelligence. Because these men function in terms of muscle, moxy, and murder, it is understandable that the Negro appears over and over in some sort of reference. (The thinking Negro has never been important to white people *or* to Negroes who live on popular culture images.) Those appearances are understandable in an era when the Negro has taken the spoils of physical engagement from the white man by the force that arrives in the symbolic arena of athletics. That might explain why Hemingway, sensing that outcome, retreated to the world of shooting, fishing, and bullfighting. In "The Light of the World," he mentions the unforgivably black Jack Johnson through the bitter recollections of a whore who watched him knock her beau's teeth out. "He'd just knocked Jack Johnson down, the big black bastard. That nigger beat him by a fluke. . . . Steve turned to smile at me and that black son of a bitch from hell jumped up and hit him by surprise. Steve could lick a hundred like that black bastard."

One by one, sports that formerly defined professional white masculinity—boxing, baseball, basketball, football, and now golf—have come to be dominated by Negroes. As blue-collar workers with guns, the criminals of *Reservoir Dogs* measure themselves in almost every way by their relationship to Negroes. In a bizarre joke early on, one of the robbers breaks up a fight between two others by saying that they are acting "like niggers," claiming they're going to kill each other—which is exactly what the white men do at the end. In our time, we can understand far better why the gun, not the fist, assumes importance as a fighting tool in film. Since Joe Louis and Sugar Ray Robinson, it has become progressively harder to imagine a white man taking down a Negro with his fists. So the white man with the big gun and the big clip comes to dominate the image of the screen hero. The world of guns and weapons of mass destruction remains the private domain of the white man, or the one in which he is superior to anyone who steps into the street looking for him.

These sorts of complexities are essential to understanding how clearly Tarantino perceives the ups and downs of race relations in our culture. He recognizes the professional relationships, the friendships, and the attitudes run through with love and hate, attraction and repulsion. In that sense, he goes far beyond any other white filmmaker who has stepped into the world of crime to tell us something about the racial and racist terrain of our culture.

In *Pulp Fiction* we are again in a world of boggled time, references to pop culture, a number of people brought together by crime, drugs, and what some consider racist commentary—even though the infamous N word is used frequently and almost exclusively by Negroes, with the exception of two white racists, who would be comical if they were not so monstrous, and a suburban nerd played by Tarantino himself. The two black main characters, each a criminal, use the term to mean many things but almost never as an insult, which suggests that whites who hear it are either insiders or people whose opinions don't concern them. Though Tarantino has been accused of racism for having his characters use the word so often, he is realistically noting how the word has changed in the conversation of street black people, who have many meanings for it, from praise to insult.

In contemporary usage and in the work of pop entertainers such as rappers, "nigger" (or "nigga") is spoken as a form of "liberation" from convention. Richard Pryor brought it to us in his standup routines but by the time he repudiated it, the barn door was open and the horses were nowhere to be seen; the epithet was everywhere. To those who use it freely and even fiercely, it means that a black world exists with its own rules in which the word is well understood in its various meanings. The purported liberation and use—even to refer to a white person—means that it is both ethnic and universal. A middle-class Negro might use it in private (with pride or disgust), but a street Negro doesn't care who hears it because he or she no longer is concerned with phony middle-class standards. This may explain why white teenagers refer to each other as niggers—they are attempting to identify themselves with those black people who use it the way they want to use it, no matter how repulsed a "proper" Negro or a white liberal might feel when hearing it on the street, in a standup routine, or on a rap recording.

This has *nothing* to do with Lenny Bruce's idea that the negative or demeaning definition of a word can be emptied with repeated use. Tarantino understands that when a street black person refers to a white person as "my nigger" he is saying that this person has crossed the line separating black from white and can understand that he or she is being saluted, not brought down to the old meanings that were stable in a world far less fluid than the contemporary one. But Tarantino does not miss the fact that racists know too, too well that there is an enduring power to the old insults. In the real world, nigger is a traditional insult; it refers to a position *down below*, which black swagger, comedy routines, and rapping have no power to change. If racists believed *any* of that theory about liberation through repetition, they would already have found another word to express their contempt, their paranoia, their hatred.

So Lenny Bruce was wrong and those Negroes whispering or chanting or shouting "nigga" here, there, and everywhere are, finally, quite naive. Tradition can reassert itself with a vengeance. The best proof of this was demonstrated in the refined pages of the *New York Times* Arts and Leisure section. Terry Teachout, a music writer for *Commentary*, used the proliferation of the word as a shrewd form of license. In an article broadly implying that Negroes were bad off because they *never* had much get up and go, the writer quoted letters of Louis Armstrong in order to call black people shiftless, lazy "niggers." This was an intellectual version of minstrelsy in which a white writer used the blackface of a Negro's words to smear the rest of the group. This is a not too distant relative of the white supremacists meetings in which rap videos are shown and spoken of as "them—not us—telling the *truth* about themselves."

This was startling, even given Teachout's history as a paternalist campaigning to put black people where he assumes they belong. What is not startling is his inability to back up his claims. In defending a dismissive *Commentary* article on Duke Ellington, intended to take the great man down a number of pegs and quiet the rumblings from the black compound about Ellington's surpassing compositional gifts, Teachout resorted to huffy ad hominem attacks, avoiding *all specific musical questions* raised by jazz scholar and bandleader Loren Schoenberg. After all, why *answer* aesthetic and musical questions about one's knowledge of a Negro's ability? We *are* talking about Negroes, aren't we? Don't be absurd. We're up here, and they're down there, and that's *that*.

In the *New York Times* article, Teachout could have easily made his point without using the epithet. But that would not have done what he wanted and it would not have defined the danger in the new freedom so clearly. It was the focused intent of a soft core bigot who had been waiting in blubber and resentment to get his chance. In Teachout's *The Skeptic*, a biography of H. L. Mencken, the writer looks at extreme statements about Jews from many different perspectives, citing various statements of Mencken's and giving a rounded analysis rather than just dismissing him as "that anti-Semite." Nothing of the sort is done with Armstrong, who had many celebratory things to say about his fellow Negro musicians and the Negroes who listened to and encouraged him. Such quotations wouldn't have served Teachout's purpose. He *might* have been itching to call black people niggers in print, but "the paper of record" would never have given him license to do so had there not been such a loosening of standards projected by rap. We cannot imagine that august paper allowing Teachout to pointedly quote a Jewish writer using the term "kike" in his letters. Would never happen.

All these complexities are implied or made explicit in *Pulp Fiction*. Here Tarantino reverses the *Reservoir Dogs* theme of a secret black–white partnership bent on bringing down a gang of robbers and killers. The professional alliance and friendship is between two hit men. Given their occupation, the friendship is corrupt coming out of the gate. The black hit man uses the term "nigga" all the time, but neither his white crime partner nor any other white uses it apart from declarations of racism or assertions of square and aggressive distance from reality, as with the suburban nerd played by the director himself. The hit men do their bloody murdering for a black crime boss who uses the term "my nigga" to draw the line between his plantation of ill will and those who work below him, much like chattel updates assigned to do his bidding—or else.

The crime boss is the ultimate extension of all blaxploitation fantasies. He has everything a criminal Negro is supposed to want: a white woman, a big house, a swimming pool, an expensive car, plenty of money, and a crew of obedient lackeys, black and white. He is not only Mr. Big; he is *Mr. Big and Black*. But that does not prevent him from being double-crossed or protect him from the moment of homoerotic rape, as southern white racists give vent to what has long been symbolized in the lynching bees attended by white men in KKK drag.

Lynchings as festivities have been thoroughly analyzed, with attention being paid to the high pitch of the ritual moment when the genitals of the Negro were cut away. In *Pulp Fiction* we see the Negro transformed from a man into "a woman" by a symbolic act of domination. The white man watching while awaiting his turn seems even more excited than the man raping the crime boss. This intertwines the sexual excitement of violence, the requisite humiliation of rape, and the desire of certain white racists to castrate the black man and sexually defile him as well. It also can be seen as an extension of the nearly erotic excitement experienced by one of the anarchic cowboys in John Ford's *The Man Who Shot Liberty Valance*. In close-up, Strother Martin, his glands bubbling up, encourages Liberty Valance as he beats down the newspaper man who has been criticizing the gunman and his gang for riding roughshod over the law.

In *Pulp Fiction* the meanings are more layered because the black crime boss is far from a good man crusading against disorder. Civilized action is of no importance to him. He will order murders and fix fights—and *anything* else that will empower him in his shadow kingdom of corruption, intimidation, and luxury. When chasing the white boxer who double-crossed him and won a fight he was paid to lose, the crime boss wounds people on the street and doesn't flinch. That they live or die or are maimed means nothing to him. He has been betrayed and that is his only concern because narcissism is essential to a criminal career, and even *more* narcissism than that is essential to becoming a crime boss. He wants revenge, no matter *who* pays along the way.

When the crime boss and the boxer end up fighting and being taken prisoner in the "Mason-Dixie Pawnshop," they have crossed into a territory of even darker kinds of violence than the American moviegoing public has become accustomed to over the past thirty years. The audience has no idea what is going to happen after these men are subdued by the white man behind the counter. Soon all mystery is removed. We are then forced into a feeling of sympathy for both the crime boss and the boxer, who killed a man in the ring and expressed neither concern nor remorse. We are taken into the basement of the pawn shop, a place even lower than the setting of earlier scenes. Both men are tied and gagged. The spiritual smut of sadomasochism gives a moral dimness to the air.

Here is the dark hell of leather, whips, shining silver metal, and torture, where violence exists for erotic purposes and the joy of domination. Here the big Negro is shown his place in the same way that the victim was shown his station in *Deliverance*—

and by the same people: hillbilly, backwoods crackers. These are not the *Beverly Hillbillies*; these rednecks have legends equal to those of special monsters. Yet these white men are not so far away; they inhabit no more than the racist wing of the murky universe in which the crime boss usually feels quite comfortable. The racist twist is that the ultimate form of domination is the white man turning the black man, as they say in prison, into "a bitch."

It is the most humiliating thing that can happen to a black man in the criminal world, which explains the lack of sympathy in the blue-collar black community for the homosexual movement. No, that is not because so many black men are criminals. Behind bars, only those considered the weakest of the weak submit to aggressive homosexual advances. Consequently the prison shower scene in *The Onion Field* (1979) makes the argument clear. Negroes tend to associate most homosexuality with submission, not sexual preference.

In terms of all of that, the crime boss could have no worse fate short of the most excruciating torture and death. He was not only slapped around by white men far below his level of criminal respect and power, he was "fucked like a bitch." Because the boxer saves the crime boss from the white men who might have gone from rape to murder after they had their way with him, the high and mighty gangster lets the boxer go, telling him not to mention the rape to *anyone* and to get out of town. Here again we have a black–white alliance but in a world so morally clouded that it is hard to find a way out of it. The two hit men open the film by murdering some young guys for the crime boss; the white hit man saves the crime boss's wife after she overdoses on heroin; the boxer kills a man in the ring, kills the white hit man sent to murder him for not throwing the fight, and rescues the crime boss from a raping pair of rednecks—killing one and leaving the other to the enraged powerhouse gangster, who coldly promises to have the "hillbilly boy" screaming from pliers and a blowtorch as he is slowly served up to his maker.

Pulp Fiction, like all Tarantino films, is an extraordinary piece of ensemble acting. The actors deliver the epic styles of speech and manner that Tarantino's talent prepares for them in a script that proves again how well he can hear across the accepted barriers of society by accepting no limits at all. The film is slowed down by the scenes with the boxer and his girlfriend. She is too coyly sweet and frail in the context of the rest of the movie. As a major surprise in character, Jules, the black hit man, is converted by what he considers a miracle. After he and his partner killed the young men at the start of the film, one of their partners burst out of another room and emptied a hand cannon at them. The long barrel almost touched their chests from across the room, but not one bullet hit either of the killers. They then shot him to pieces. Later Jules concludes that his life in the world of crime is over because "God got involved."

This is the only spiritual conception of any sort in a universe where killed or be killed, get or be gotten, screw or get screwed are the only rules: the "real" world is too far below heaven to work in any other way. The references to the Cain character in television's *Kung Fu* fit perfectly into Tarantino's understanding of how deep human reactions can be inspired by pulp; those who experience such reactions may only be able to describe them to others in the lingua franca of pulp. The *Kung Fu* series that premiered in 1972 set the tone for the American fascination with martial arts and lightweight aphorisms purporting to reflect the Asian sense of spirituality in an opaque, demanding universe. That is our version of the aforementioned chinoiserie, the European obsession with Asia that held sway in the courts and the homes of the aristocracy a few hundred years back.

Jules may have decided to wander like Cain in *Kung Fu,* but his travel is intended as a mobile form of waiting for God to tell him what to do with his life, which is about as Christian as you can get. God is not inside of him; God remains *outside,* in control of an infinitely large plan and a place for every person willing to seek the truth. The contradictions of predestination and free will do not obtain; those contradictions are more a matter of language than faith, which achieves sense through revelation, not logic. Those kitschy Asian references allow Jules to explain his change of heart, but that odd American mixture of superficial external influences is held in place by a black Christian perspective. This is how most Negroes in America spiritually relate to the outside world, even in the Nation of Islam, which purportedly despises Christianity as "the white man's religion" but delivers its own message in the pulpit style of the black American church, where a fresh version of exaltation was invented. The influence of the Nation of Islam is alluded to in the disgust that Jules feels for pork, describing the pig as "a filthy animal." The Nation of Islam had no serious religious impact on black Americans, but its sustained attacks on the pig were felt as a good number of blacks, even hit men like Jules, ceased to eat pork, which meant that beef ribs started to take their place in the Negro world of barbecue. Tarantino's use of that detail in the character of Jules supplies us with another example of how well he knows the worlds from which his characters emerge.

None of that, neither the change of heart about murdering people nor the decision to seek his spiritual destiny, impresses Jules's partner, who hilariously expresses the sense of ongoing privilege that black people often witness when traveling with whites into one social situation after another. His white buddy shows no respect for the house to which they bring a body after an accidental and very bloody killing in their car. Jules reprimands him when he leaves the hand towels stained red as they wash off the gore in the bathroom. When the two of them need a favor, the white guy gets smart with the man sent by the black crime boss to get the hit men out of trouble. As he and Jules clean the car in which the accidental killing took place, Jules finally blows up after his partner complains about how everyone is trying to walk all over him. Jules also has taken some guff in pulling the two of them out of a mess. This is not unusual, but the obnoxious way the white hit man reacts to normal situations demanding a bit of humility is a very funny version of the sense of white privilege that is legendary among black people.

Amid the black comedy, heartbreak, and shock of this narrow world without heroes and without morality, the spiritual needs symbolized by the black hit man's quest arise. It is understandable that his character chooses to change his ways because, in a manner of speaking, black people have lost the most in the reduction of the world to no more than sheer material. The unsentimental power in the singing of Mahalia Jackson and the oratory of Martin Luther King Jr. has been eroding since the era of blaxploitation and the cultural rise of the hoodlum. Once assumed to possess a formidable connection to the deeper meanings of spiritual life, black people have been so debased by the images of pop culture that they are no longer thought of in reference to an enduring spirituality. No such force enters the area of existence where Tarantino's characters love, plunder, are duped and dispatched with an emotionless cruelty. Using the deracinated language of pulp in a deracinated culture, the troubled hit man tries to rise though the purple membrane that encloses his world. We have no idea whether or not he will make it.

The two volumes of *Kill Bill* tell us about how closely Tarantino watches this culture and how well he understands the female fantasies of our moment. Neither film can be separated from what has happened to women, white women especially, in this period of reinvention—or reassertion. *Kill Bill* is about the blonde woman warrior, an all-American daydream. The initially drab look of feminism evolved into something quite unexpected, as mixing health and politics resulted in toning and weight loss and suggested that men and women had no differences other than their genitalia. Up in here, what do you expect? This is America. Self-defense was the next step because no modern woman wanted to spend her life seated on the cold, cold bench of potential victimhood. Women started studying martial arts and trained as boxers. In the pink or the brown or the yellow, they were quoted as saying that it felt good to experience the sensation of strength and to feel far less afraid when walking the streets alone at night.

New careers expanded the range of available female images. The rightful pride that women took in law enforcement and military service added figures as new to our cultural landscape as the corporate woman who figured out how to be herself without submitting to a butch style of dress that obviated her femininity in the interest of *pure* business. Yet when one addresses all of that and is well aware of how many white women have been physically intimidated by those occasional knuckleheads among the minority of black women on college campuses or an equally small number among high school students in public places, one can understand—without defending it!—the fantasy desire to put that pink foot in a black heifer's ass. Volume 1 of *Kill Bill* immediately speaks to that dream.

The fantasy has its own black foreshadowing. Everything comes back to roost, covering the clay heads of our myths with chalky excrement. In the blaxploitation films of the 1970s, the black heroine always got revenge for the humiliated Butterfly McQueens in the seemingly endless versions of the dummy

mammy in *Gone with the Wind* or *Duel in the Sun*. The black heroine had to do it; it was time. She had best slap the hell out of a
white woman or give her a good beating or, best of all, send her
to the graveyard while self-righteously letting the devil woman
know that *this* black woman here was no maid, no mammy, no
intimidated black bitch who could be dismissed as irrelevant.
She was an African *queen*, mother of the universe, ready to bust
some boodies and take some names. Like her man, with her
head held up high and crowned with a globe of black wool, she
was *superior* to these weak-kneed, pampered white bitches, and
was plenty ready to prove it with her fists and her feet. The
white woman had been mighty only when the black woman was
tied down. It was time to back the fuck up and leave a cloud of
dust while doing it. Or else. Yeah: or else.

   That melodramatic image ignited the anger of black females
who were being flanked on every side by the white female competition on college campuses that began on the heels of black
power as black students started to go to northern colleges in
larger numbers than ever. Like John Henry, the black woman
was thwarted by technology. She couldn't stop the laying of rail
tails or the laying of pipe. The birth control pill and the IUD
removed the fear of pregnancy and helped produce the cultural
conditions that prevailed in the 1960s and 1970s, which can be
summed up as "drugs, pretensions toward Eastern religion, and
unbridled interracial sex." Though hardly any ethnic group can
be called erotically provincial, black men and women *both* were
at that time. White women were not. They were ready for just
about anything, and if they weren't and if it wasn't painful, they
got ready for it. They read about sex practices the world over and
absorbed books like *The Joy of Sex* because they were determined not to be the bad lovers or unimaginative boudoir
women they assumed their mothers were.

The blues came home when black men from coast to coast were experiencing varieties of sexual pleasure that were defined by black women as nasty, even filthy. The willingness of white women to experiment with missionary zeal and learn about the endless degrees of sexual pleasure through this new set of standards put them ahead of black women for years. Their willingness took away the crown of natural sex queen from black women and left them with no more than a can of Afro spray and a hair pick. Worst of all, the black woman became a symbol of sexual limitations, and white women who knew what the deal was looked on them with a new kind of contempt or even pity, which was all the more infuriating. Black women were harder to get than white girls and they were too conservative when they finally took their clothes off, or so said many young black men who were no longer willing to put up with women who were always ready to challenge their manhood and almost always looked at them with disgust when they asked for some sexual pleasure that might not be in the unwritten black version of the Victorian sex code. It was one thing to be considered less sophisticated than white women who might have been better educated in private schools and all *that*; it was another to find themselves alone in their dorm rooms steaming over how white girls could wag their fingers and have black men come drooling after them like mindless hounds.

Ironically, the "unnatural" sex acts that racists had long warned white women against experiencing with black men—the beasts—were now performed by the young, alabaster and pink and chalky and freckled Christian and Jewish females of America with the special intensity that always arrives under the banner—or the bed clothes—of rebellion. Through sheer performance frequency those acts soon became natural and so did clitoral stimulation by men, even reluctant black men who had long considered oral sex proof of a lack of masculine power, a way of making up for a bad or mediocre performance, a white man's first line of defense for being a sad sack in the sack. The most unexpected result of all was that competing with white women for black men *actually led to the sexual liberation of black women*. In consciousness-raising classes held for black women only, the word went out that they had to give up their Victorian attitudes toward certain sexual acts and get on their knees and give the white women a stationary run for their money. By the early 1980s, the Victorian vision central to the sex lives of black women was gone and the boudoir battle was *on*. Women were united across the color line: *everyone* was giving it and getting it, too. The page had been turned.

In no way did sexual liberation remake the idea of the white woman in the world of physical action, of self-defense, of returning to her pioneer heritage. Though there were changes. Beginning with Mary Tyler Moore on television, she learned to live alone and earn her own keep; she made the climb up into the corporate world; she became an expert technician. She got out of the kitchen, off her back, stepped from behind the stroller, and became much more than a matriarch or matronly or sexless or borderline lesbian female who had no chance in the heterosexual world. In *Friday 13th, Halloween,* and *Romancing the Stone*, perhaps the three most notable examples, the white woman *saved herself* and set a new precedent for action and horror films in which the female fights off the villain or *kills* him. Hell hath no fury like a woman about to be murdered.

Memorably, in the *Alien* series the Ripley character took the pioneer woman into the next frontier, outer space. But those were marginal characters and marginal heroines. There were no females who had the success garnered by Charles Bronson, Clint Eastwood, Sylvester Stallone, Bruce Willis, and Arnold

Schwarzenegger. Not one white female star ever became as successful as Pam Grier did as an action heroine in those blaxploitation films. What was the route back to the white woman's
pioneer imagery, real or imagined?

Quentin Tarantino knows. Let loose a wronged white woman,
a killer, who will kick the most ass ever kicked on film by *any*
white female and see what they think of *that*. Let her crush rep-
resentatives of every ethnic group in the democratic sweep and
superiority of her fury. Will the public love that? Oh, yes.

Though he had begun talking with Uma Thurman about
making *Kill Bill* during the filming of *Pulp Fiction,* part of its
impetus may differ from what he admits in public or Thurman
herself fully understands. It could be the result of his choosing
to switch from a black to a blonde lead because it gave him a
chance to brilliantly snicker at the taste of the public for surreally
absurd violence *while* weaving his inevitably complex commentaries on our time—covered, as always, by the dense mask of
cinematic allusions. Allusions are the food of educated fools.
They fail to understand that a work of art—whether tragic or
comic or a mix of both—might be enriched by the summoning
power of allusions but is never given its deepest authority by
them. If all Quentin Tarantino did was feed the flies who devote
entire Web sites to the discussion of academic droppings, he
would be of no importance. He knows a good deal about America, as I have been saying all along, and he has never stopped
knowing what this nation is and why. Even when combined with
styles as far removed as the impossible Samurai battles of *Kill
Bill*, there is always American business to be taken care of, which
means we have to understand this latest bloodbath and love
story in terms of the one that preceded it, *Jackie Brown.*

No matter what he says about it, it is hard to imagine Tarantino not being hurt by the less than celebratory response to his

masterful *Jackie Brown*. In *Jackie Brown*, he took Pam Grier, that empress of blaxploitation, and gave her a chance to show what she could do. She never had that opportunity in the laughably clumsy black films that made her famous but were no more than icons of bad fashion, bad writing, and barely competent direction. Grier did not act in those films; she only needed to show off her epic chest, smile, scowl, look bemused or thoughtful, deliver the bad lines, and kick some white ass in a couple of badly choreographed sequences. The person on the receiving end of her wrath was a white woman, a drug dealer, a white gangster, or some Uncle Tom who had sold his soul to the white folks.

Jackie Brown was a rejoinder to all of that. With Tarantino authoring the script and working as the director, Grier seemed to get more screen time and more close-ups than any black actress could expect in an American film. She responded with a performance so filled with variety and nuance that Tarantino must have been pleased with how far the result was from anything she made during her blaxploitation days. His choice was to create a film that worked as a comment on the limitations of blaxploitation: his heroine was human, a flesh-and-blood thinker who defeated the bad guys—as well as cops working against the bad guys—by calling on her wits. No choreographed fight scenes, no faux black nationalist mumbo jumbo, no popping cleavage or shower scenes. Sure, there was plenty of sexual innuendo that arrived through Grier's easy charm and warmth but no molten kisses, no hugs, no shaking of a bubble butt. Jackie Brown was no genius but she was also nobody's chump. Her goal was to outfox the guys who stood in her way. She intended to make a new life for herself. Jackie Brown had lived a hard life in a tight rut. Her vitality had been worn down but it had to rise through the fatigue and uncertainty of a woman in her middle forties who had learned long ago that good looks did not guarantee her anything of value.

Reading the novel on which *Jackie Brown* is based, Elmore Leonard's *Rum Punch*, reveals how far away from blaxploitation Tarantino was aiming. *Jackie Brown* is a character study, a movie of racial manners, and another attempt to make the bad guy human while remaining a monster. In the novel, the character called Jackie Brown in the film has sex with the bail bondsman who aids her in duping the white cops and the black gun runner. Not up in here. There is always an underlying eroticism and banked heat that never comes out fully.

Tarantino chose to remove most of the novel's shoot-outs between the police and the bad guys and challenged himself by substituting the emotional range of his people for the special effects and adrenaline pumps of cinematic bloodletting. There is also a reason for not making the female lead a white woman. He did this so that both central characters could be black and the audience could be shown how this man and woman related to each other and to the white people who surrounded them. This made it possible to explore his theme of black and white working together for the interests of civil society and black and white working together *against* society. Ordell and his crime buddies sell the firearms that make hells of America's cities. Jackie Brown, a flight attendant for a small airline, has been snitched on by one of Ordell's accomplices. The cops and the feds pick her up, knowing that she smuggles the gun dealer's money to his hiding spot in Mexico and brings back whatever amounts of cash he needs. The cops and the feds aren't interested in Jackie Brown; they want Ordell.

Samuel L. Jackson plays Ordell and brings enormous repositories of detail to one of the best roles the great actor ever had. Spike Lee and some others were upset by how often the character used racial slurs, but they were absurd. This is a *character*. Ordell is the sort of slick, crude Negro who would *never* edit himself. For him, "nigger" is a universal word and can refer to black people or *anybody* else. Going far beyond Elmore Leonard, Tarantino made him into one of the most perfectly conceived monsters we will ever come across. Ordell is an extension of Drexl from *True Romance*. Ordell is the real thing and just as ruthless, and he is also funny, very funny, especially when explaining something to his slow-witted white crime partner or threatening and dominating his blonde surfer girl (each of which is given an exquisite and unpredictable reading by Robert de Niro and Bridget Fonda).

This variation on black and white teamwork is more complex than what we saw in any previous Tarantino films, including *Reservoir Dogs*. But there is a characteristic balancing of numbers. Jackie chooses to work with the white cop and the white federal officer. Ordell has to use his white crime buddy and his aging bunny of a surfer girl. Three versus three. Jackie Brown, however, has an ace in the hole, the white bail bondsman Ordell sent to get her out of jail after she was busted at the airport. He is willing to help her do anything she wants. Jackie Brown and the bail bondsman (played with plenty of understated gravity by Robert Forster) work together against both the law *and* Ordell. Ordell is a menace and a murderer, but the law has to be fooled so that Jackie can give the guys with the badges their man while getting away with the $500,000 Ordell earned through illegal gun sales.

In a blaxploitation film, Ordell would have been the hero or a tragic hero who wants to get out of the game but cannot make it in time. In *Jackie Brown*, he is, first of all, a killer with ice water in his veins. Yes, he wants to get out of the game, but when we have to choose between him and Jackie Brown, our sympathy goes with her and we feel no tragedy when she tricks him into a situation where the cops gun him down. Dead as Dillinger. Earlier in the film, Ordell had murdered a black accomplice who had been arrested and knew too much. He jeopardized Ordell's game and had to be shut down for good. To keep Ordell's mouth from mucking up *her* plan, Jackie Brown has to make sure that he cannot tell the cops that she has the money. As they sometimes say in the undertaking business, "Could be you. *Somebody* got to go."

As usual, the language is the light, and so much of the remarkable street talk and the insights that arrive in that form of American speech lift *Jackie Brown* far above your ordinary heist drama. It is a thriller that has very little on-screen violence. Tarantino didn't want anything to startle the audience. His intention was to get people to listen and look at the subtle nuances of vocal tone and expression in the face of Pam Grier and give a listen to the many shadings of Samuel L. Jackson's voice and how well he works his eyes, the turn of his mouth, and the tilt of his head to underline, expand, or bring contrast to the words. Like Grier, he is a master of expressive silence.

Grier is exceptional in her role because she does much with what some consider the cool, uncommitted surface that is a legacy of slavery, from the time when black people had to see terrible things and give the impression that they were not touched or did not sympathize with the person being beaten or packed up and sold off. It is the Negro version of the stiff upper lip, and it has taken on a quality of dismissal over the years. Having a command of that posture and knowing how to signal what is going on underneath is no minuscule task for an actor. That is why we are moved by the way Grier stands in an almost stereotypical black posture, fronting as though angry and imposed on by the law while projecting the fear and the nervousness of a black woman who feels, behind the bravado, that she is pinned to the cotton and about to be crushed. She says almost nothing in court when she is brought in from jail, her hair undone, glamour vamoosed. Jackie Brown is possessed of dignity but is clearly frightened because the only thing heard in her mind is the sound of a future sentence she cannot handle at this point in her life. Her moments of exhaustion tell us a lot about what she has been through, and we understand how little life has given her when we watch Jackie wistfully listening to the Delphonics sing "Didn't I Blow Your Mind This Time?"

The song is from the 1970s and becomes the theme music of Max, the bail bondsman who is smitten by Jackie the first time he sees her. It is not nostalgia. Max has never heard the song before but he buys it because it reminds him of Jackie's vulnerability and toughness as she stood in her bath robe listening to the music as if there might be a place, somewhere, with that kind of feeling set aside for her. A foolish dream, sure, but one worth having.

The Delphonics, in the harmonic gauze of a keening rhythm and blues ballad, evoke a romantic set of meanings and inclinations that have been cast aside by the aggressive, hedonistic vision of rap, which opposes romance and love, just as Ordell does. This is very important. Tarantino does not let us believe for a second that Ordell sees women as anything other than toys, pets, and servants. He has too many dreams in his head about retiring and spending his gun money, hey, to give any special thoughts to women. If a woman can provide him—or one of his buddies—with sex, entertainment, maybe do some smuggling for him, fine. If not, he couldn't give a tinker's damn in a town without tinkers. Well, he does draw a line. He would prefer to have his favorite surfer girl—who's not good at sex but is kept around because she's white—be busted in the mouth instead of shot and left dead in a parking lot. But if you have no choice, you *do what you have to do*. The most important thing is that such a difficult bitch does not *live*, which would result in some people being sent up the river, long enough to believe in forever.

Part of the brilliance of this character study arrives in the shifts of mood that we witness when Jackie is talking with the different white characters. In conversation with the cop and the federal agent, she doesn't quite beg but leads them to believe that they have all of the cards, that she is afraid of going to jail (which she is, by the way), and that she can sweet-talk Ordell into the trap they are setting for him. They are wary but they believe her. With the bail bondsman Jackie is strong in a way that would neither frighten nor disgust a tough man whose help she needs to pull off her sting. But she also gives the impression that as well as needing some help, she needs *his* help. With that, baby, the two of them can turn Ordell into a slice of bacon on the grill of the law and—watch this—make off with half a million dollars. The bail bondsman is taken by her sense of this being her last chance. He is impressed by her ruthlessness, feels sympathy for her palpable fear of coming out, again, holding the wrong end of the stick. After all of that, the bail bondsman is knocked to his knees by, well, the implacable and seasoned beauty of this woman, mussed up or fixed up. Doesn't matter. Not only does this happen the first time he sees her, it loses no force in moments of fear and doubt as he voices his concerns. He listens very carefully to Jackie's plan and moves through it, always carefully, always aware of the consequences if they are caught.

Robert Forster gives the details of those reactions in his eyes, the set of his face, and the warmth that comes into his character's voice when he speaks to Jackie Brown. The tone is very different from the world-weary contempt he has when speaking to Ordell. The door he keeps closed while running his business slides back and a renewed person appears. We see a man become enthralled in the way he always dreamed of—by a woman deserving of his willingness to never say anything to her other than "yes." I don't think we have ever seen this sort of passion felt by a white man for a black woman without one word being spoken, the emotion itself being the "back story." There is plenty of sentiment but no sentimentality. She is not seen as a jungle or an urban goddess; the human density of her spirit and her charm are enough.

The relationship between Jackie Brown and the bails bondsman is paralleled by the one between Ordell and Louis, Robert de Niro's character. A master, de Niro makes Louis obviously dim-witted but never overdoes it. His admiring friendship with Ordell is unique. The white man has to cut through the tough exterior of the Negro and find the good person within, or he is somehow elevated by coming into the black orbit of life, which is, inevitably, portrayed as ultimate version of the vital. Ordell and Louis are criminals beyond redemption. They are bottom feeders in a lake of thick slime made gooey by the blood of the those already murdered and those who will be murdered with the illegal guns for sale to anyone. Ordell is not some clichéd, hip, street black man come to lift up the spiritually refrigerated white man and teach him how to get the good foot, actually both feet, on the hot groove that will allow him to sweat down his socks. Ordell is a demonic figure who seems large of mind because he is surrounded by dull-witted types. His vision is petty, but theirs is pettier. This convinces Louis that Ordell has it all going on, even though Ordell's surfer bunny cuts him down to an unbelieving Louis whenever his back is turned. The scenes between Ordell and Louis are crafty and insightful, played out with feeling for a character who loves to preen and another who loves to watch him do his stuff or impart his wisdom, even remove the hood of good cheer that reveals his membership in that closed club of those who murder without conscience in order to keep their businesses running smoothly.

In *Kill Bill,* volume 1, Tarantino provides us with a true inside joke that, if I'm right, went right over the heads of his critics. As one woman said to me recently about *Charlie's Angels*: "Are we actually supposed to believe that these very small women can dispatch men over two hundred pounds so easily?" Well, no, but supposedly hip white women and third degree cliched feminists of all colors believe it does the souls of women good to "see a woman kicking ass." Perhaps they should be aware that such films ought to have a warning at the end: *Don't try this on the street.* In no physical discipline—from boxing to martial arts—does a good little man beat an equally good big man. The power and the weight behind the blows always determines the outcome. Even the greatest boxer of the twentieth century, Sugar Ray Robinson, would have been beaten by Muhammad Ali. He could not have withstood the blows. Tarantino understands that so well that he makes sure the battles are fought with Japanese swords, supposedly the most deadly weapons in history, but so light that we can imagine a woman being fast enough with one to do a man in with her speed and that razor edge. Such a possibility reminds us of how important technology has been to changing the position of women in modern society.

In *Jackie Brown* Tarantino showed us how absurdly the "equalizer" (firearm) can be combined with feminism and right-wing fascist "ideals" such as Timothy McVeigh's: "kill them all." Immediately following the title sequence, the black gun dealer and his dull white friend are looking at a video on television in which the Statue of Liberty is shown firing an automatic weapon into the air, with the "Star Spangled Banner" blasting, rock guitar style, in the background. Lady Liberty is pressed into service as a symbol of mindless, paranoid power, a domestic version of Saddam Hussein in green stone. It is the beginning of a gun advertisement featuring a blonde in a red, white, and blue bikini, with a body builder's arms and form shooting an automatic weapon. The blonde is followed by a sequence featuring other white bimbos in two-piece swimsuits who blast away and talk about their favorite automatic weapons. In this way Tarantino brings together corrupted patriotism, fascism, female body building, and the individual's weapon of mass destruction. Jackson delivers a monologue that makes clear how many black street criminals are influenced by the kind of weaponry they see their antiheroes using on the silver screen. That the film he refers to is Asian provides a link to *Kill Bill.*

Kill Bill, volume 1, neither reaches such levels of grim satire nor the depths of Tarantino's bawdy, comical, and violent essays on American identity. It is not intended to. Tarantino is after what the audience wants these days—a cartoon in which somebody white breaks *everybody* else down. It is sort of a "Sheena, queen of the jungle" set in America and Japan. It uses the normal American formula of subjecting the lead to so much violence and humiliation that, when the time comes, no moral consideration of any sort need be shown to the villains. They can be dispatched by the most gruesome means imaginable and the audience is supposed to say, "Right!"

Kill Bill is made powerful, however, because the lead is played by Uma Thurman, who is one of our greatest film actors, and can always come with it. She can deliver the purity of *any* emotion. Every feeling of unmentioned interior hurt, every sob in the middle of battle, every expression of physical pain is made real in soft or big red letters. Her sort of wonder is what most action films lack, the feeling that in the middle of this surreal, absurd bloodletting a living woman is taking the pain and giving the pain. Her actions are nothing other than inverted heartbreak. She is the rose stripped of everything except the thorny stem. That is her identity. In her luminosity, Thurman perfectly embodies that American idea of "rights" transferred from the world of the law to the code of the abyss. "I am in pain and somebody *has* to pay for this. I have that *right*." Without Thurman's genius for close-ups, making her face an instrument capable of giving us levels upon levels of emotion, the film would have no resonance. Her humanity carries the movie and gives it the kind of elevation only a great actress can, which is the same force that lifts any American genre film into art.

In the genre context, *Kill Bill* seems like a shrewd joke. Tarantino combines the things we see in fluff like *Charlie's Angels* with visually exciting but pretentious works like *The Matrix,* where the quality of appetite being met is pretty obvious. In *Charlie's Angels*, we get a bubble gum expression of the primal action fantasy of white females *right now,* which is to equal white men in their ability to best the opposition—even on their own turf, even in their own style. The fans of the *Matrix* love how the film goulashes together Eastern and Christian religion and philosophy as a justification for the necessary killing that expresses the "rage against the machine" that has been in our consciousness since the middle of the nineteenth century, made most explicit by Mary Shelley, whose *Frankenstein* has taken on greater and greater dimension ever since, especially now with the threats that ripple through DNA research, cloning, and the cyborgs of the future. With the Industrial Revolution, human beings began to feel themselves shrinking in the shadows of expanding technology and became ever more paranoid about that overshadowing. Symbols of the trouble move from the innovative handgun to the repeating rifle and the weapons of mass destruction, in which mountains full of stockpiles are turned into cannon barrels and triggers become buttons.

Set a tech to stop a tech. Tarantino is not one to give much attention to the two-bit mysticism of *The Matrix* because technology or the ability to dupe the masses with it is not the real problem. It is always abuse. Far too much of what we learned since the printing press and have used to fight disease comes from technology. The artist must always do battle with the shallow, unless he is using the shallow to reveal its appeal and its dark powers. The filmmaker must make his statements in the world of surfaces.

As Tarantino is well aware, film, like photography, painting, and theater, is about giving resonance and history to surfaces—presenting a surface that contains qualities of revelation or allows for developing revelation. That is why there is always more going on than shines off the top. Our fluff is no exception. In *Charlie's Angels* Cameron Diaz is given a moment to show that that she may be blonde as all get out, but she has some very hot stuff. That hay-colored stuff is so full of *burn* that it can triumph in unexpected places. Right there among hostile, "show me" Negroes, this blonde can get on the dance floor, smoke away all doubt with her booty wiggles, and come out the queen of rhythm. When done, she gets all the high fives and slapped hands a white woman would want in a loud, black joint—the purportedly ultimate dance floor test. In *Kill Bill*, Tarantino does them one better. The second scene puts forward a much more provocative white female fantasy. That dream, as alluded to before, is to put a foot in a black woman's ass.

In a middle-class town called Pasadena, California, in a simple home, a furious fight begins, as it did in *The Manchurian Candidate* (1963). The moment the eyes of the black woman meet those of the white heroine on her porch, they get murderously nasty with each other. In *The Manchurian Candidate,* we got the regular old white man's fantasy, as Frank Sinatra, in one of the first instances of an American hero resorting to martial arts, beats down a huge Korean villain. This has nothing to do with the kind of improvisation we saw from little Alabama up against the big Mafia goon. It said that, given a sliver of a chance, our man from the superior land of Caucasia could wipe out *anybody, anywhere* in the world. The code name for that fantasy among black wags was once joked about as "the mighty whitey syndrome." The natural history of the syndrome preceded electronic media and was an extension of dime novels about Indian killers and gunfighters. In the real world, long before Muhammad Ali, John L. Sullivan declared, "I can lick any man in the world." The world today may be much larger in every way, but in the symbolic universe of popular art, that vision is rock steady, and Tarantino plays with it in *Kill Bill.*

   The epic opening battle of punching and slashing and kicking and crashing has an ominous background because these are two former members of a team dominated by female assassins. The black one is apparently retired and living a bourgeois life that is a wide awake dream on the other side of many murders; the blonde is out for revenge because she was shot in the head as the team of assassins murdered everyone at her El Paso wedding, where she was in advanced pregnancy. Until recently the blonde heroine lived a nightmare version of the Sleeping Beauty fairy tale. In a coma for four years, she lay in a Texas hospital where her sexual favors were sold to anyone who could afford to sneak in, pay off an opportunistic hospital employee, and squish while no one was looking. The sleeping beauty of assassination suddenly wakes up to find herself on the receiving end of a rapist, whose tongue she bites into and stretches before she finishes him off. Tarantino's love of turning time around in his narratives is why this scene arrives *after* the blonde knocks on the door in neat and sweet Pasadena.

That opening battle of blonde on black is interrupted when it reaches a vicious pitch—or bitch. The black character's daughter comes home from school in a yellow bus that lets her off outside of their home and right in front of the yellow "pussy wagon" owned by the slain hospital worker who was selling the blonde's body. This is one of Tarantino's snapshot commentaries. Little girls may travel to and fro in yellow school buses as they are educated, but their crudest destination in our culture is "the pussy wagon," a symbol that declaims the American female blues in which a woman, however learned, is considered no more than an anatomy.

Some say that existentialism can be reduced to the idea that existence precedes essence. The loud yellow truck says that the very word "pussy," among the most barbaric men, precludes the essence of individual female personality. Even as she lies in a coma, with no personality on display other than an unconscious muscular reflex of spitting, her vagina gives her value as an opening for sale, one that, detached from any response, can be lubricated with vaseline if it becomes dry. Her hole is her entire story and the source of her brutal degradation. When she awakens and keeps her eyes closed as she listens to the orderly explain to his customer that she is not to be bitten or bruised, only used for $75, her rage begins to simmer and we are expected to realize that the number of times that she has been mounted and slobbered over and had monstrous things whispered into her ears is an unknown succession of callous encounters. The coma creates a blank past of being prostituted, the hospital room becomes a sex shop in which she is turned into a warm, flesh-and-blood version of a plastic sex doll, a sperm receptacle for male fantasies of masturbation. The only reason this dead-to-the-world blonde has been spared beating and mutilation is that the marks would show and bring the business to an end. So she is more than a bit hopped up when she gets to Pasadena. Whether this is supposed to be real or a fantastic dream is obvious. To let us know that we are only looking at a movie, the raging, awakened Sleeping Beauty repeatedly slams the door of her room against the head of the fallen hospital attendant as he lies with his temple next to the door jamb. His head neither bleeds nor swells. Odd. Could Tarantino not have noticed this? Doubtful.

After the door of the yellow school bus door opens in Pasadena, we see a black girl walking to the house where the two women are posed for a wary moment in the middle of their death dance. The stylized hatred between the races has finally risen to the top. On entering the house, the innocently beautiful black assassin's daughter sees the results of the titanic destruction of middle-class order as the two women threw each other into glass tables and furniture. The girl is intimidated and surprised at seeing her mother and this strange white woman. Each of them is hiding a knife behind her back, both are shining from sweat, faces bloody, with their hair all tangled, and neither one is talking right. The girl, suspicious because she knows something is wrong, is sent to her room.

In the kitchen, the female warriors take a break from trying to kill each other with bread knives and skillets. They talk in the manner of black street women, as though they share the same background, and similarly verbalize contempt or threat or boast of a hard time already zeroing in on the opposition. The black character bitterly tells the white woman that, back when they worked *together* as killers, their boss, Bill, had the nerve to give the white girl the nickname of "black mamba," which should rightfully have been *hers*. This moment presents the main theme, appropriation, the good or bad effects of which are nearly always central to what Tarantino is probing.

The black woman's anger is a reversal of the white woman's desire. White women want to be equal to black women because the postmammy black woman in America has long served, in the popular imagination at least, as the *full* female, the one who can completely depend on herself if she has to, get up off her rusty dusty and go into the workplace, pull her own weight, leave smoke in the sweaty air of the dance club, drive a man mad in bed when the time comes to get hot, sweet, and tender in the freest ways. If necessary, this woman will defend herself to the death rather than take any bull dookey from *anyone*, high or low, on the face of the entire goddam earth.

Slavery and racism, we have been told, demanded these strengths of the black woman. She stepped up because she *had* to step up. As the blonde matches the black woman insult for insult, surly tone for surly tone in *Kill Bill*, Tarantino is flipping over contemporary identities and laying out the drive for appropriation as an answer to the malaise of whiteness. Traditional whiteness is the enemy in nearly every way to whites who consider themselves hip or are trying for the cool of the moment. As we find in *Thirteen* (2003), even the shape of whiteness is no longer as highly regarded as it once was. *Thirteen* is a film about teenage white girls, who inform us along the way that the black female physiognomy has brought another model to our standard of beauty. We see that young white girls are especially happy if they possess "ghetto booty." Watch out now.

It is important to *Kill Bill*, volume 1, this satiric paean to Caucasian fantasy, that the blonde does in the black woman at the start of the movie. This herds in the white girls and lets them feel that sense of being taken, once again, to the front of the human line. This is a blaxploitation moment in reverse. Everything is established for the blonde action hero with the power of the choreography and the distance from reality. Blood is always capable of gluing together the world of myth and reality; it brings together the fantastical deaths of mythic heroes with the grime of murder that leaves its large or small cuts, big or little holes. Red: the ultimate symbol of fire, of anger, of violent death.

The knives are very important in this moment because they represent the pure sort of close contact that blades always denote. They are also important because Viveca A. Fox looks buff enough to tear Uma Thurman apart if they were going bare knuckled. The way she shakes her head and says, "Come on, bitch," as they move into the living room before they are interrupted is an unresolved moment of pure threat. No ordinary white woman of Uma Thurman's size—unprepared in the gym or the streets or somewhere—could stand up to *that.* The black woman's death is spectacular but willfully phony. What kind of an ex-assassin is she? The woman pulls out a hidden gun and, at close range, *misses* her target. If we didn't know it was a fantasy before then, we would have no doubt from that point forward. We are going to be bathed in a blood shower and the one giving the shower is the blonde, who is also known as the Bride.

Tarantino, alluding to a 1993 article by Tyler Jones, has said that he sees action movies as similar to musicals. *Kill Bill,* volume 1, fits that description except that there are other things pushed under its violent surface. There is the ongoing idea that one should never risk being taken in by a refined presentation in a white dress, even the dark sweater and plaid skirt of a schoolgirl. Everything can conceal, or cover over, a killer. You better look closely because you might never understand how near your throat is to a razor or your head is to a gun barrel.

This is made clear when the theme of miscegenation rises into its full position. We encounter it when we find out that the two most highly placed women in the supreme Japanese criminal organization are half-castes, one part Chinese American, the other part French. In her droll voice-over narration, the blonde tells us that they have literally cut down the competitors. There is celebration and all of the crime council members are happy except for one, Boss Tanaka, who is outraged because the council has chosen to let a half-breed female head their beloved organization. The newly appointed crime boss runs down the banquet table and beheads him. Then she becomes as she was before, almost coquettish, but makes an essential point. She will, from time to time, listen to those who respectfully question the logic of her actions, but anyone who has the audacity to discuss her race or her blood as a negative will lose his fucking head. In this council of murderers, Tarantino makes his point once more. At its purest, democracy means that *anyone* can rise to the top— even a woman in organized crime, the most extreme end of a sexist society where women *follow* orders, don't give them.

The central anyone is the blonde, who proves to be too much for the entire personal gang of the half-caste crime boss. Her professional skills as an assassin, the heartbreak she suffered from Bill's crew, and the trip she made to Okinawa to get a special sword from Bill's master have all prepared her to be the final butcher of the blues, the snuff angel of reckoning, the flesh-and-blood human being who endures whatever pain of combat she must in order to fully become the yellow-haired pulse of death. None of this, however, is to be taken seriously or literally because that would make its surreal dimensions no more than absurd. It is a wild nightmare and fantasy.

The dream quality of the film is intensified by the creation of multiple time periods that work together inside the narrative and spread it out in aesthetic directions that go far beyond a stack of quotes. This is Tarantino's vision of the many miscegenations of humankind expressed through a polyglot of cinematic styles. In the world of the arts, this goes back a bit in terms of major creators. Wagner was preparing to write an opera about Buddhism when he croaked, and James Joyce toyed with the implications of the West moving toward the East. Duke Ellington, when introducing his "Afro-Eurasian Eclipse" in 1971, cited Marshall McLuhan's observation that the West and the East were moving so close to each other that soon neither would be able to easily recognize itself. "Now it is hard to tell who is enjoying the shadow of whom," Ellington concluded. Tarantino is out to prove that he is in his own cinematic way, creating an original, celluloid chinoiserie. It is now a long time since Marco Polo or the French and Dutch ships traveled into new kingdoms of design and human style. Now *all* styles belong to *everyone* and those inspired to the most inventive degrees will render them with penetrating authority, for drama or fun or a mixture of both.

In Tarantino's moving picture world of contemporary gangsters, everything is modern *except* their weapons. They drive cars or ride motorcycles, talk on cell phones but never use guns. The crew of Bill's killers who shot up the blonde's wedding seem to be in an American time. When the blonde travels to Tokyo, she enters the mythical time of samurai combat and the traditional past becomes part of the present, slicing and hacking its way out of the grave of history to arrive in our moment, ready for blood. This is the lopsided era of the rising sun, where old and new create contemporary discontinuity. There it is *always* earlier than it is in the West.

Like the acrobatic sword-wielding male heroes of old Hollywood such as Douglas Fairbanks and Errol Flynn, the blonde battles her way through all of the human obstacles between her and the queen villain. The bitch empress of Tokyo crime wounds the blonde across her back in the final duel and makes light of this arrogant white heifer by saying, "Silly Caucasian girl likes to play with Samurai swords." She apologizes for being so nasty when the blonde comes back and slices the leg of the crime queen. Everything is complete at this point. The blonde has killed the black woman and the raping white guys, she has traveled to Okinawa and gotten a retired sword maker to forge her mighty weapon, and has done away with the Asian hordes of the mob queen's private army in Tokyo. In conclusion, the blonde, bloodied but not bowed, slices off the top of the half-caste female crime boss's head. Even though she apologized, the woman had mentioned the blonde's race in a negative manner. The blonde has now proven herself deadlier than the male and superior in skill to the Asian. That's a lot of fantasy for one plate.

As already noted, *Kill Bill* cannot be removed from the democratic aspirations of our time, which remains, as I once called it, "the Age of Redefinition." We should not be surprised to know that Japanese flamenco guitarists have won competitions in Spain, Negroes have been television stars in Japanese soap operas, the giant Yao has appeared to challenge fellow giant Shaquille O'Neal in the NBA, a half-caste like Tiger Woods—part Asian, part black—dominates golf, Chinese American Jeanette Lee, "the black widow," runs professionals off of the pool table, and the Williams sisters have used their unprecedented talent to dirty the tennis shorts covering the rear of the game, kicking all white ass willing to step on the court. That is the underlying theme of this silly Caucasian fantasy in which Tarantino creates the first white female star whose level of slaughter equals that of white action heroes such as Sylvester Stallone. Don't forget that Stallone returned to Vietnam as Rambo and seemed to kill enough Vietnamese to make it impossible for that country to wage war until a generation had passed.

Kill Bill, volume 2, is another animal altogether. Everything is stripped down because the blonde has but three people left to kill, though she only kills one. Bill's brother is bitten by a snake hidden under a million dollars in cash by one of the three on the list, a woman with a black patch over her eye. She is not killed by the blonde, who prefers to pluck out her remaining eye, leaving her sightless and sputtering threats, no longer dangerous to anyone outside of her black kingdom where, one imagines, she will remain "visually challenged" until another term for blind is invented.

We get the blonde's story and it is quite something. She was trained in China by a martial arts expert, went out on jobs for Bill, and left the murdering organization when she found herself pregnant by Bill and wanted to start all over, with a new name and a new life. Bill thought she was dead, killed in the field of a business that does not guarantee missing in action notifications or proof of death. Bill felt loss and grief that taught him the immeasurable dimensions of his love for the sweet, tender killer blonde. He became quite angry, even irrational, when he discovered that she was still alive and planning to marry a clown of a man in El Paso. Then came the Greek anger, the slaughter, finished off with Bill busting a cap in the blonde's head.

In volume 2, Tarantino slows things down and moves from the emblematic to the personal, granting his characters plenty of face and talk time. Thurman, who often delivers a performance in Volume 1 much like the one Pam Grier gives in *Jackie Brown,* with the pain and the fear just below the cool surface of the skin, is let out now, and shows us love defiled and the hard martial arts training she received in China at the behest of Bill, the

suave pimp of female killers. Along the way, Tarantino introduces us to an almost beguiling Mexican whore runner. He was
one of Bill's mentors. In a tone just a bit stronger than matter of
fact, he tells the blonde that he would not have shot her for trying to run away. No. He would only have cut her in the face.
Long after the pain was gone, any mirror would remind her of
the extent of his rage. She would understand, in the pimp's
logic, how much he had been disappointed when he took a top
money maker and turned her into a gargoyle. We see exactly
what he is saying when a woman serves them drinks and the
bride looks at her face, which is deformed by a cut down the
middle and across her mouth. She is a degraded symbol of the
pimp game, wearing the scarification of its code.

Martial arts and pimping are the two disciplines that Bill has
brought together; they form his version of miscegenation, his
corrupt duality. Martial arts is built on a vision of honor in
combat, of strength, speed, cunning, and the suppression of
pain. The study is bent on turning the body into an instrument
of the will, brought to a razor's edge by the strop of hard study;
it allows one to face the demands of combat with the resolve
and confidence that transcend anger and viciousness. Its origins
are defensive, but like everything in our world, it has been corrupted by aggressive rather than defensive uses. The profession
of pimping has no honor and cannot be corrupted, only slop-
pily revealed in its essential brutality. Every idea we have about
women—as sisters, lovers, mothers, and individuals worthy of
respect—is mashed down by the greed and exploitation that
drive the pimp's game. Psychological manipulation is used to
send women into a degrading, dangerous profession where they
are paid for their favors but could be abused by loons just because they are willing to sell themselves. Sex in any imaginable
version is not all the job can entail. Down the darker lanes, any-

thing can be asked of them—as long as their clothes are not dirtied and they can go on to the next customer. The place where all light is replaced by hatred could easily be the point at which they will be beaten, cut, or murdered. If his whores are not willing to risk encountering the pathetic and the monstrous people who lure them in with money, the pimp has to step away from sweet talk and the promotion of a faux partnership in which he and they take care of each other. When they balk at going to work for him or conclude that they are not in a part-nership, or are caught holding on to a bit of the loot for them-selves, the pimp has to let all of his "bitches" know who's boss. He has to be willing to beat them down and take the position that *they* gave him no choice.

The blonde has worked on the most harrowing plain of prostitution. She has sold herself as a murderer, not a sex worker, though we have no doubt that she or any of Bill's other girls would put herself in a sexual position if her assignment demanded that she get that close to the target. This is why the morality is so twisted. As David Carradine has said, there are no good guys. That is the point. When Bill warns his brother that the blonde is coming, he responds that for what they did to her they all deserve to die—but, *so does she.* She is no angel but her suffering has made her one. Sort of. Tarantino is working from a premise that filmmakers discovered years ago: once the out-numbered killer is pursued by the police and the film cuts back and forth between this lone man and dozens of cops, our sym-pathy floats to him, unless he has done things so horrible it is impossible for us to feel anything other than the hope that the killer is caught or executed, on the run or by legal means.

As in *The Road to Perdition,* we are never shown the killer at work. All of the blonde's killing for Bill remains off-screen. We do not witness the things she did that got her such a tall reputation. So we make no judgments of her that would fit into the context of conventional morality. We see the blonde enduring attempts by Bill's boys and girls to kill her. Her revenge on them makes everything "even steven." We see the blonde facing the excruciating disciplines of martial arts training at the hands of her Chinese master. We eventually question that part of her schooling. We wonder, since he has also taught Bill and seems to have taught all of his girls, if the master himself is corrupt, selling or offering his services to any who are willing to accept the physical demands of the discipline. Does a willingness to suffer cancel out the intentions of the student? Does a deadly art remain the same in the profession of a killer? Does a student's talent and fortitude remove all moral responsibility from his or her teacher? These questions, like the smoke of a fire down below, slowly rise through the floorboards of the narrative.

We see that the blonde is indomitable. She will take on and kill any number of people to taste the bitter satisfaction of revenge, the violent forest in which one can become lost and end up the slave of murder instead of its master. Tarantino turns a corner when the blonde becomes pregnant and decides to get out of the game because she does not want her child to grow up under the overcast sky of that profession. But she does not escape the profession or her identity. This is made clear when the blonde finally meets Bill, who has taken care of their daughter for four years. As Bill tells his former lover a story before he dies at her hands, we hear a tale implying that her daughter has the merciless virus in a small frame. The little girl has taken a goldfish out of its bowl and killed it. The only reason appears to be the fun of ending a life, a small one, but a prelude to a larger appetite that may be inevitable. In the end, one must be who and what one is. Bill tells the blonde that she cannot turn away from her calling, which is slaughter. The haunting implication is that someday she will face the force of murder as it appears in her daughter, which will be the proof that life—the undefeated killer of people and their illusions—will get you if nobody else is strong or cunning enough.

The only neon weakness comes near the end. Through early flashbacks, we see the blonde training in China under a a master to whom Bill has sent her. We learn why she is able to smash her fist through the wood of a coffin after she is later buried alive. In one flashback Bill explains that the great Chinese master has a martial arts technique that will cause an opponent's heart to explode within a few steps, but he teaches it to NO ONE. Since we do not see the technique until the end of the film, we are not surprised when the blonde, disarmed by Bill, uses it to dispatch him. Had she suddenly called upon this strange martial arts move, we would not have understood what it was. Were we then to see Bill telling the blonde about it in flashback, the last stroke of the final battle would be more satisfying. So would the brief conversation that precedes Bill's death when he rises and walks his last few steps.

The satisfactions remain on multiple levels. All of Tarantino's themes are brought to the film as a whole. There is loyalty and betrayal, corruption from the top and from the bottom, false or deceptive surfaces, a pulp sense of life stripped of its purple characteristics by the feeling of the characters—and we have the perpetual theme of miscegenation and partnerships that cross ethnic and sexual lines, cultures and traditions. It is improbable that Quentin Tarantino has exhausted himself or his audience or the comical nerds who know not what they see because they view all of his work through the blinding lens of allusion. He is a major force in American art because of how well he understands the interplay between the human themes that are as old as the species and the omnivorous strengths and weakness of a popular culture that defines itself by borrowing, extending, appropriating, and defiling. Above all, no one understands better than he the many miscegenations that make our modern world the unprecedented thing that it is.

Thus all of Tarantino's themes are brought to the film as a whole. There is loyalty and betrayal, corruption from the top and from the bottom, false or deceptive surfaces, a pulp sense of life stripped of its purple characteristics by the feeling of the characters. We have the perpetual theme of miscegenation and partnerships that cross ethnic and sexual lines, cultures and traditions. It is improbable that Quentin Tarantino has exhausted himself or his audience or the comical nerds who know not what they see because they view his work through the blinding lens of total allusion. He is a major force in American art because of how well he understands the interplay between human themes that are as old as the species and the omnivorous strength and weakness of a popular culture that defines itself by borrowing, by appropriating, by defiling. Above all, no one understands better than he the many miscegenations that make our modern world the unprecedented thing that it is.

Blues To Go

I WANT TO CONCLUDE THIS BOOK ON THE PROBLEMS OF authenticity by adapting and expanding some comments I made to literature professor Nibir K. Ghosh, who teaches in Agra, India. This out-chorus, this getaway, this final wave of a gauntlet is intended to ball itself up and should, if I'm successful, retire the opposition team and send it back to the dugout, where all clichés belong. For *this* inning, at least.

In the Ghosh interview, I went into some detail about writing and writers in a way not touched on in this volume until now. I spoke to issues not only in America but the world over, or the world over as I understand it. Our own troubles with authenticity can inspire us to look at problems that arise in and out of our country because I truly believe that the American future is the future of the planet at large. We continue to grapple with the many problems of freedom, which means that we must address integration on every front. Integration is demanded of us and has been demanded of this nation from its inception, regardless of the bigotry that sustains the variations on tribalism that are at the root of xenophobia, the universal villain of a thousand masks, many of which have been and are still being stripped away. There are very complex relationships between xenophobia and visions of identity that arrive across our national lives and show themselves up as versions of dilemmas and victories. As we examine these relationships, we see things that have international implications, that demand a maturity when we scrutinize the heritage of Western literature, that call on us to cut through the Gordian knots of cross-influences, and that provide us with models from our own literary history that can we can use to build our own ships and take sail on the blues-dark sea of experience.

As a nation, we find ourselves confronting a set of clichéd conceptions based in the narcissistic concerns of the public—its weight, its looks, its vacations, its income, its spiritual concerns, now so frequently shifted from the world of faith to that of fast food from the gods. The interweaving of appetite and creature comforts has begotten industries devoted to specialization that could inspire high-quality fiction. That is because the story of precision, as it arrives in the individual life, is an aspect of experience that we do not share with the great past, which was dominated by craftsmen, not precision engineering (which has a unique meaning in our democracy).

When we are not focused on the narcissism that arrives when "the pursuit of happiness" is established as a democratic goal, we love the scandals. They tend to humanize, shock, and breed contempt. Yet another set of ideals can either be mourned with great sentimentality or dismissed as further proof of how superior cynicism is to any other kind of assessment. I prefer what I call tragic optimism because the model of medicine is most appropriate to our kind of democracy. Tragic optimism does not expect to perfect men and women. It assumes that folly, corruption, mediocrity, and incompetence are the demons who arrive season after season if we are talking about human beings. That, like the disease and death faced down by the world of medicine, is our tragedy. Our democratic optimism comes from the proof of our ability to learn and to fight until our learning takes notable position in our customs, our policies, and our laws. But many, like the spoiled child for whom nothing is good enough, prefer cynicism. Yet it is a very limiting way to look at things, especially for an American. Cynicism can never make much of those human moments that prove the power of the species to hold onto its humanity even when seemingly unprepared for some horror too large and too unfamiliar to handle with a set of reactions already warmed over, waiting in the oven.

September 11 is a perfect example. Right here in ice cold New York, where everything is thought to be impersonal, regimented, and defined by rudeness and disregard, the people of this town rose up against a massive murder raid with the only hope that the species ever has. Color, religion, class, and sex became secondary to the tragedy in a way that can only be described as spontaneously noble. New York ran its true colors up the international pole of electronic media on that monstrous day. It gave the world an example of all that can be done— which is to reach out and do whatever you can for someone you do not know and for no other purpose than to express the depth of your empathy.

Two things about Manhattan and this country emerged as subjects writers need to ponder. September 11 in New York had the quality that Hollywood handles so terribly when it wants to show the oneness of humanity. All of those people in downtown Manhattan, where hell came from above, not below, were covered with brown dust and transformed into a single wave of endangered, suffering humanity. As far as I know, all were helped without regard to who or what they were. The second most remarkable reaction was nationwide. A basic and hard-won democratic respect was shown toward Muslims, who were not subjected to the kind of hysterical mass murders we would have seen if the situation had been reversed, with men like Timothy McVeigh flying hijacked passenger planes into Middle Eastern targets. Any available Americans would have been slaughtered. No one can argue that.

At the same time, we have to realize, if we are actually concerned with human possibility, that the Muslims who murdered and publicly burned the bodies of three unarmed American businessmen in Iraq are no different from the white Americans posing with pride or glee in the indispensable *Without Sanctuary*, a photographic documentation of American lynchings. One particularly revealing picture is from 1935 Fort Lauderdale, Florida. In it we see pretty little white girls, probably accompanied by mom and dad, staring up at the strange fruit of a garroted black corpse. Once the irrefutable horror, tragedy, and madness of those photographs have been absorbed, an unexpected emotion can set in. It seems to me that we ought to feel great pride in a country that came such a great and difficult human distance in seventy years. If the Islamic world is lucky, it will evolve equally as far beyond its present tendency to hysteria, something no American should have the nerve to pretend has never been a monstrous strain in our history. The point is that the democratic belief in the individual lifts him or her out of the symbolic category, the target board for murder that we have so many examples of in our own nation.

These are the sorts of things a serious writer has to contemplate, whether what is made of them has no smell, a sweet aroma, or a stink. It is a complex dilemma for an American writer, and it challenges so-called minorities with a special complexity because the great writer from the past can fail some of the tests demanded of one who writes in the wake of the civil rights movement and the fall of colonialism. Something big can be addressed in one place and something disturbing can appear someplace else.

Take Thomas Mann. Mann wrote *Lotte in Weimar: The Beloved Returns* to examine why the German personality had a predilection for totalitarianism. Discovering that novel remade my sense of the extra-literary. I realized that someone who has sufficiently mastered the craft of fiction can make things work that might be dismissed when handled by others. This was very important to one who had come of age in the 1960s, when surpassing victories were achieved for human recognition beyond color but were countered by the imbecilic, tribal ideas of black nationalism. Then it seemed to me that all of *Joseph and His Brothers* was, essentially, a protest against anti-Semitism organized as an astounding orchestration of historical fact and the legend of Joseph. Mann proved that the artist can make a complex set of statements about life and all of its meanings while consciously stepping on the bugs of bigotry that cover the floor as they rise from down below.

To write that book while the Nazis were gorging themselves on the intellectual and spiritual carrion of xenophobia was no less than a marshaling of the forces of the novel—not so much for good as for cleansing the human palate or pumping the collective stomach. The artist cannot always tell you what is good to eat, but he or she should recognize what constitutes poison. By concentrating on the foundation of dreams and the meaning of forgiveness—which is one of the highest aspects of civilization—Mann made a hero of himself through the expression of a deep integrity. But there was more. The bestial images of Negroes in Mann's work are a long way from

James Joyce's *The Dead,* in which the character Freddy Malins is described as having listened to "a negro chieftain singing in the second part of the Gaiety pantomime who had one of the finest tenor voices he had ever heard."

That problem in Mann is not only true of European Genius. Due to the unfortunate influence of the Nation of Islam, through Malcolm X and Louis Farrakan, gullible Negroes were marched into a dubious sense of unambiguous unity with the Arab world. That world was described as an alternative to the frustrations of American life; it was a paradise free of racism and bigotry. But the truth is known to put its foot deep into the crack of delusions. Many misinformed Negroes were shaken to learn that Arabs *still* sell black slaves, whom they consider inferior. One need only examine the contemporary abolition movement documented on iabolish.com to see what is going on and to understand through interviews with black Africans what *unreformed* Arab attitudes toward them have been and far too frequently *are right now.* Of course, this is *not* a matter of genetic determination but of cultural attitudes. These can be seen, as Playthell Benjamin pointed out to me, in the first story of *A Thousand and One Nights.* The bestial descriptions of black men and the sexual paranoia are right there. If Sir Richard Burton's translation is accurate—and we have no reason to think that it is not—then we might have the first classic racist descriptions of black people—the images that would be taken up by Thomas Mann in the high German air. In *A Thousand and One Nights,* those descriptions appear in conjunction with the sexual fear of black men and the idea that Arab women could become slaves to their tools and lose their minds to debauchery. Ooo wee. Ooo wee. Or should I say, "Ooo, wee wee"?

Clearly Mann's vision of human life and human value had precedents in Europe and beyond. Mann seemed to stop at the skin surface. This sort of thing demands maturity from ethnic and female outsiders who want to be free of simplemindedness. They must handle one rough and ready fact: the one who makes a great contribution might have no place for *you* in his vision of society, but that does *not* diminish the dimensions of the gift. This helps one avoid being sidetracked into rejecting more than *should* be rejected. The example I always give is that no amount of public information about William Shockley's racist attitudes toward black people is going to make Negroes stop using transistors, the invention for which Shockley and two other men received the Nobel Prize. The transistor is one thing, Shockley is another. Anyone who fuses them is being very, very foolish. That's how it is. For those great contributors with bigoted limitations, one must always be ready to say, "Thank you and fuck you very much."

That applies to everything of value and includes the contemporary problem of discerning the difference between improvising on influences and so-called "appropriation," which is only defined in one direction by those who impose topical politics on the arts and make an industry of it in our beclouded academies. Beginning with the eighteenth- and nineteenth-century Western fascination with the Far East, this tendency to go outside of one's tradition has led to romantic ideas about the Middle East, which was known as "the Orient." This evolved into the twentieth-century conception of being "a citizen of the world." Taking up external influences and making what one will of them led to Picasso and others being naively accused of ransacking "traditional" African societies to replenish Western art. That is the kind of naïveté that amounts to nothing of value for a writer. Style has laws that move no further than the form itself; whether one likes it or not, styles are not ethnic franchises. In today's world, they may start with ethnic origins but grow into unpredictable international inspirations.

Given the higher aspects of the American Negro's original remaking of European sources, as one example, people need to calm down and face the facts. Expression is the issue; color is never the problem in the world of art, comprehensive recognition of humanity is. The origin of inspiration is irrelevant. We writers who use the English language cannot get past Shakespeare because he is still the greatest master of it. Giant-killing Will used his craft, as Harold Bloom says, to "invent" the human, to give us an epic understanding of the human heart and mind. But if some untranslated Third World person has given us more to build on than Homer and Shakespeare, trot him or her out here and get to work. Time's a-wasting.

For all the low-grade political prattle and academic hustles, ours is a time when some writers are going beyond limitations imposed by shallow politics and shallow readings of history and culture. They sense that civilization is the issue. As far as I am concerned, there is no other issue. Civilization means something quite different than it used to because the vision of democracy continues to purify the bigoted provincialism of the Enlightenment. As we can *now* understand it, civilization is *always* at war with xenophobia, which can arrive in folklore, religion, politics, philosophy, phony science, and the popular arts as well as the fine arts. Writers have to recognize xenophobia in its many forms in order to avoid uncritically betting on a particular color or a particular history. To understand Hitler in context is invaluable. It will allow one to lance the intellectual boils and let the sentimental pus run out.

Hitler was the last of the formidable and self-declared tribalists; he embodied the great demon of xenophobia. But men like Stalin and Pol Pot were of the same cloth. Latin Americans have known these things for a long time, even if they have flirted with the narrows of Marxism because it sounds so goddam good on *paper*. Novels such as Alejo Carpentier's *Reasons of State* and Gabriel Garcia Marquez's *Autumn of the Patriarch* (an extended improvisation on the film *Citizen Kane*) set high standards for the examination of dictatorships and the cultural complexity composed of Indian, European, and African mixes. The Chinese who went through the Cultural Revolution know what a monster Mao was and how easily—or cleverly and dangerously—xenophobia can put on the mask of communist revolution, dehumanizing and murdering those it defines as opponents on the basis of class and education. We can be sure that China will produce its own Milan Kundera and give us the human meanings of totalitarianism in a Far Eastern mode.

Africans who create their own killing fields along tribal lines are part of the same monstrous crew. Rwanda is no joke, nor are those rebel kids running around with guns and either mutilating or kidnapping girls who become sex slaves. These are supremely brutal children, no more, no less. Color has nothing to do with it. Whatever they are, these savage young men are *not* embarrassments or proof of African inferiority. They prove that Africans are human, just as the endlessly bloody Greek myths make clear what human beings have to fight against in order to arrive at a civilized level of understanding. African writers are now challenged to go beyond propaganda, the blame game, and the fear of feeding stereotypes. They have to deal with their backward ideas about women, their corrupt military dictatorships, and tribalism—the father of all racism. In that regard, Nuruddin Farah's new novel, *Links*, is an important contemporary work because he stares the African dragon in the mouth and spares nothing, African or not, as he looks into the rampaging mysteries and horrors of Somalia. Good for him and good for us.

As writers, we also have to deal with the legacy of St. Paul, which is that a terrible man can transform himself irrevocably. This *also* happens or there would be no hope for our species. We *can* learn. If that were not true, the kind of horrific public spectacles documented in *Without Sanctuary* would still be acceptable. But we can also *pretend* to learn in order to slip the noose. As Woody Allen observes in *Crimes and Misdemeanors*, we can do terrible things, feel guilty about them for a bit, then forgive ourselves and, as they say, "Get on with our lives." These are the complexities of our moment, and only the most serious writers will step up to them. That is why I believe the serious writer is the servant of civilization. The hard questions must be asked, the human heart investigated. An endless job. Not one for those given to yellowing their underwear.

These issues of the human heart and mind take on particularly ironic relationships in this nation. Influences flow back and forth as well as around and around, touching everyone or providing material that is adapted and sometimes defined as coming from one ethnic group when it actually began in another. Writers who are aware of this can make far more telling observations about American life. For instance, the greatest crisis that has ever faced the black community is the present disengagement from the world of education, which is embraced by more and more of the lower class, the underclass, and even the middle class. Defining discipline, study, eloquence, punctuality, and taste as "white" or "inauthentic" creates an absurd play with a Negro cast.

Here again we find confusion about authenticity. All of those ideas are not expressions of untrammeled black cultural purity; they are totally white in origin. Anyone who looks can trace them back to the anti-intellectual rise of a "common man's culture" that began after the War of 1812. The desire was to beef up the common man and present his down-home "purity" in worthy opposition to "putting on airs." Popular art produced fictional and real figures so exaggerated in their adventures they might have been hatched from eggs of fiction. These figures were lifted up as antidotes to the overrefinement of the European. Brother Jonathan was the commonsense New England farmer and the fictionalized Davy Crockett was the rowdy braggart, the proud roughneck. The fantasy Crockett's claims for greatness might well anticipate the endless braggadocio of rap: "I can walk like an ox, run like a fox, swim like an eel, yell like an Indian, fight like a devil, spout like an earthquake, make love like a wild bull, and swallow a nigger whole without choking if you butter his head and pin his ears back." Give the rapping neocoon a coonskin cap, a corn cob pipe, and a cracker barrel. He deserves it. Origins are all.

Interestingly, this was foreshadowed in the late 1960s, when Franz Fanon's fellah (from *fellaheen*) was depicted as the pure, angry peasant, unawed by colonial power and standards, the human foundation of revolution. This character crossed the water in Fanon's *The Wretched of the Earth* and was soon—in line with the most naive and omni-directional American love of rebels—turned into "the street brother." This "rebel with a black cause" was particularly important to black American college students from middle-class backgrounds. *Finally*, this group of Negroes had its biker, its rebel with no respect for "white" middle-class values. This "street brother" has had a number of manifestations—the Black Panther, the street hustler, the rastafarian, and, with Tupac Shakur, the pure thug with sentimental pretensions to sensitivity. This was a "corrective" culture defined by blaxploitation.

In this poisonous iconography, there is no room for a Frederick Douglass, a Bessie Coleman, a Thurgood Marshall, a Duke

Ellington, the Tuskegee Airmen, Ralph Ellison, Marion Anderson, Charles Hamilton Houston, Vivien Thomas, Leontyne Price, Dr. Ben Carson, Wynton Marsalis, or any of the black people, male and female, who have risen from somewhere down below. Their efforts to master a craft have brought them inarguable distinction. They are not just models of behavior but models of possibility and inspiration for a fresh line of short stories and novels. The sky is the limit. Consequently the opposite view—this redefinition of black authenticity all the way downward—is a new kind of American decadence excused by many Negroes because of the money it makes for a handful of black polluters, onstage and offstage. The crudest, most irresponsible vision of materialism is fused to a naive sense of how far one can go in the world even if illiterate and unskilled. This too is marvelous material for fiction because it involves interplay with media, status symbols, and many aspects of American life.

The irony of influence is central to the American tale, of course, of course. For that reason, writers shouldn't be surprised to find that the *national* appreciation of full, round buttocks is not only new but may be the only significant cultural contribution to come out of rap (which puts high value on, as L.L. Cool J said years ago, "a big old butt"). This has *always* been true in what Langston Hughes called "the quarter of the Negroes," but now it has been nationalized (perhaps internationalized!) by those ignorant, misogynist knuckleheads down there with their gold teeth and their updated minstrel outfits. No matter what we might say about them, they have surely expanded what is considered beautiful in this nation and that, my friends, cannot be dismissed, primarily because it shifts the way women relate to their mirrors and to traditional standards of good looks.

The film *Thirteen* (2003) showed that there are young white women in possession of robust backsides who no longer see themselves as too fat or deformed or some such. They now celebrate that fleshy characteristic and pridefully speak of themselves as having "ghetto booty." I think the term "ghetto" is unfortunate because it denies the existence of such specifically gorgeous globular flanks among black woman above the lower class. In a culture that defines authenticity from the bottom up, it is understandable that such a shift in cultural definitions of female beauty would be defined by class rather than ass. Few things in America come out of nowhere, however. I have often wondered if the nineteenth-century bustle was a foreshadowing of "ghetto booty." These things provide the writer with fresh kinds of grist.

Black authenticity is a theme so mixed up with social motion that it needs to be examined in its true context, which goes all the way back to slavery. When Africans first encountered the strange black go-betweens assigned to ease the transition into slavery, they immediately realized that those men were dressed and carried themselves like no one they knew back home, as Nathan Huggins made clear in *Black Odyssey*. Later every black person who became educated and took command of the English language seemed mighty goddam white to those left in the plantation environs of chattel slavery. The Negroes who went to the black colleges begun after the Civil War were not "authentic" the way their unlettered brethren were. In *Huckleberry Finn*, we see another angle on authenticity. Huck's drunken father is outraged by a well-spoken, natty Ohio Negro who knows more than one language and carries himself as if born free but should—by all rights!—be up for sale at a slave auction. In James Baldwin's *Just Above My Head*, his black New York kids are on a gospel tour and go south, ready to fill buckets with crocodile tears as they experience how southern racism has degraded their brothers and sisters. They encounter a monied southern black middle class that, far from sitting on cotton bales and plucking banjos, looks on them as mere black trash from northern slums.

That is part of the American tale of unpredictable upward mobility and movement into careers that were once possible only in the unbigoted land of dreams. It is an American story that we all share, even the "mission Indian" who was changed by mastering the white man's ways. Another version of this appeared many years ago as Barbra Streisand talked to Golda Meir on a television show that allowed Hollywood to express its nationalism by saluting Israel's fortieth anniversary (something I sincerely doubt would get beyond a single meeting today). Streisand's attempt to impress Meir by being cute, funny, and charming in a Hollywood Jewish way made big Golda seem to think, "Tell this girl to start singing. That she does well. She must stop talking. This girl believes *nothing* is a good subject for conversation. The world should not know we in Israel are related to this silly person."

We should understand from these examples that the threat of becoming *trivial* lies before us all. It is the iron shadow in which all ethnic groups and both sexes tremble. *That* is surely a subject for good American fiction if it wastes no time on the expected sentimentality, self-pity, and self-loathing that do *not* take us deep into the souls of characters. We are, however, in an ongoing metamorphosis. Tracking that metamorphosis is one of the jobs of the ambitious American writer. My attitude is get into it whenever you can. Writers should be aware of this shifting American shape and resist the idea that it will result in the American waking up one day as an insect.

One example is Andrea Lee's *Interesting Women*, which has gracefully expanded the canvas of our fiction by placing black female characters in European situations where they function in the upper reaches of society, not as desperate concubines or show ponies. I think this is new. One of her best stories is about how some servant-class black women in Madagascar challenge her protagonist and what she has to do in order to let them know she is not about to be run over, even if they are so beautiful, so primitive, and so "authentic." *Drinking Coffee Elsewhere*, ZZ Packer's version of *Dubliners*, is a "moral history" that introduces young Negro men and women, most of whom are not poor but remain helpless in the post-civil rights era as they attempt to meet the contexts of their moment and satisfy their dreams. The failures of prepared ethnic revenge, the strategies of the Christian church, the educational system, the cartoon pomposity and ethnic worship of black nationalism, and the defensive masks of aloofness define their limitations. Try as these characters may, they cannot run away because there is no place to run that will allow them to become more than the sum of their spiritual shortcomings and their longings. These tales form a literary blues of defeat, what Joyce called "paralysis." If Packer's emotion ever fully meets her gift for detail and her splendid ear, she might send most other writers running for cover. *Daughter* is a sharp and powerful first novel by asha bandele. It presents fresh psychological insights against a simple racial incident that becomes, in the process, far less simple, as do the lives raised into three dimensions by the writer. The short story writer Dana Johnson is a black woman who has lived among American white folks and perceives the many different levels on which racial encounters take place, or do *not* take place. With will and luck, she will achieve her apparent intention, which is to bring these circumstances alive the way Balzac did the class nuances of Parisian life in the nineteenth century. Snooty white critics and Negro writers addicted to diatribes and self-pity have a parallel misunderstanding of these matters. We should expect *more* complexity and *more nuance* from fiction that goes down into the valley of of the basically untapped ethnic subjects that have been before us for years but have inspired so little literature.

As writers, we need to pay close attention to these new black people who have grown up in the world of overt cross-cultural influences that define part of the post–civil rights era. Such people, from the suburbs or integrated environs, seem more white than black to those held down by a narrow conception of authenticity. (We have already seen this problem taken to the mat in Barbara Probst Solomon's wonderful *Smart Hearts for the City*, when the heroine's Jewish identity doesn't fit the borst belt model.) Detractors need to get their watches fixed. That is something we *all* have to get ready for, and make the most of, because it's not going to change or recede, no matter how wildly Negro females fix their hair or how many Africanesque trinkets successful black men wear, no matter how many of these new Negroes give African and Arabic names to their children.

Let us hope that writers, black or white or whatever else, begin to take on the idea task of drawing sophisticated three-dimensional black women who arrive on the page as something more than deracinated salt pork in the greens of clichéd attitudes about refined black people. There are so, so many contrary examples but so few characters that make my case with the power of art. For some time I have wondered why Toni Morrison makes so little of the black female experience that she knows in person. Oprah Winfrey and Leontyne Price are supposedly two of her best friends. Each woman soared from humble beginnings to conquer areas of life that have been touched by few people of any color in America. What they have lived and know and must talk about goes far, far beyond the fictionalized gossip that forms the basis for a lot of fiction. But

Morrison prefers to keep her characters down on the farm, and we are still waiting for the hot mama who has high thoughts. We might have hoped that Erica Jong would have brought her forward, but she didn't make it. Still, you never know. Since the exciting woman with an exciting mind is everywhere in our society, she should show up on the page any time now.

In order to do our best with the lives that stand before us, we always have to go back to the basics. We should look at the possibilities that come out of our American tradition. We should, if it fits our purposes, "write out of American literature," as Ralph Ellison said of himself. So I will end this essay with a few observations that I think might contain something of value for the writers of this nation. They provide a running start for all participants in the race that never gets to the finish line, only lets new people into the pack if they are fast and strong enough. Of course, that too must end. Our collective fate is that we ramble around and around until the butcher called time cuts us down.

Here we go. F. Scott Fitzgerald. One of his surpassing accomplishments has never been mentioned or understood, as far as I know. As observed elsewhere in this book, Albert Murray described Fitzgerald's *Great Gatsby* as the most famous novel ever written about "passing," or presenting oneself as having an ethnic origin other than the actual one. That novel is also a marvelous example of the use of the blues and a very instructive example of how to transform popular materials into literature. Fitzgerald was the first American writer to use blues as a foundation for motific development: the lyrics of "Beale Street Blues" contain almost all of the themes of the novel. That is why, in chapter 8, he mentions the song. He writes, "All night the saxophones wailed the hopeless comment of 'The Beale Street Blues' while a hundred pairs of golden and silver slippers shuffled the shining dust." That constitutes what I call a compound allusion by also referring to James Bland's "Oh, Dem Golden Slippers," and Yeats's "Song of the Wandering Aengus," which contains the spirit of Gatsby, of the obsession that will destroy him (earlier Fitzgerald referred to this poem with the words "the silver pepper of the stars"):

> *I will find out where she has gone,*
> *And kiss her lips and take her hands.*
> *And pluck till time and times are done*
> *The silver apples of the moon,*
> *The golden apples of the sun.*

William Faulkner is to American fiction of the twentieth century what the Melville of *Moby Dick* was to his, the greatest innovator and the most impressive adventurer. Faulkner's sense of ethnic conflict as a thorny fact of American life and a metaphor for the troubles of human life at large have yet to be surpassed. He remains, as Melville did, a solitary sequoia. Hemingway taught everyone the poetic resources of prose fiction in English, which explains his importance. In that respect, no one has gone beyond *The Snows of Kilimanjaro,* which is superior to all of his novels, if you ask me. It's not a short story; it's a miracle, perhaps the greatest long poem written by an American. It is fiction and poetry so perfectly aligned that the reader knows by the end that he or she has been in the hands of genius.

Richard Wright is of fundamental importance. His entire *Black Boy* (or *American Hunger* as he wanted it titled) is a major American autobiography in the tradition of Frederick Douglass. I know that Ralph Ellison read the entire book in manuscript, not the truncated version that the publishers released. I know this because the old master told me so when I pointed out to him the similarities to his novel. Ellison surely had Wright's book in mind as the foundation on which he built *Invisible Man*. Ellison lifts so many of the older writer's themes and experiences into an original world of fiction that reading them together is quite an experience. I do not think Wright had the same level of eloquence we experience when reading Ellison, but he surely had equal fire and a deep understanding of the fear that made so many Negroes tremble and held them captive, a fear that was close to what Faulkner called "the iron cold" in *The Wild Palms*.

In a certain way, Wright anticipates the writing that came of experiencing the Nazi death camps while reaching back to the gruesome clarity of Isaac Babel. That is a very hard area to inhabit because deep suffering can easily slide into sentimentality or overstatement. The sheer brutality of racism that Wright expresses with so much observation and so much fire and sorrow is a major contribution. Even if you don't like the overall effect of a given work, there is always the fact that when his characters are struck or tortured, he makes you feel it as part of the universal information about pain that we so often attempt to avoid for fear of losing the morale of confidence in civilization. Ducking the horror that is upon us all is surely Albert Murray's insurmountable limitation, for all of his greatness as an American thinker. Wright, however, makes it clear that civilization is never complete as long as it accepts the disgusting treatment of a scapegoated group—always there to pay the price of society's irrationality and disregard.

Ellison is indispensable because of his *literary* concern with what our nation is, has been, and might become. With Saul Bellow, he stands as the greatest thinker our fiction has produced since 1950. His thoughts are profoundly composed of vernacular materials, the ideas expressed in the international world of art, and the implications of our social contract. In chapter 9 of *Invisible Man,* he brings together the common man symbol of Charlie Chaplin and the surrealism of the blues with the "blueprints" of American society—the Declaration of Independence and the U.S. Constitution. It is one of the high points of our literature and a supremely brilliant extension of what Melville and Joyce showed could be done with popular materials, and that jazz musicians did with the Tin Pan Alley songs they expanded with improvisations that gave those show tunes melodic, harmonic, rhythmic, psychological, and emotional range and intricacy far beyond their original renditions.

James Baldwin's great achievement was inventing a new version of English by bringing together the sound and sentence structure of Henry James with the rhythms of black church rhetoric and song as well as the rhythmic reaches of blues and jazz. It was a major victory. Even though he decayed into a bitter and repetitious propagandist, his contribution when he was on his own special beat can never be condescended to or sneered at. That's like licking your tongue out at a cobra: if you get too close you will receive a bite to build a death on.

In conclusion, my final piece of advice, especially to the younger generation, is the sort that I got from the examples of Ralph Ellison, Albert Murray, Saul Bellow, and the neglected Leon Forrest: go out there and find something that you want to talk about and see if you can achieve an original, uncontrived perspective. Don't be afraid to face the human facts about any group or persuasion or cause. Learn from the best writers the world has to offer. Keep writing until you recognize your own sound, rhythm, and feeling showing up on the page. Always, no matter where you learn it—from the alley to the academy to the penthouse—do as they used to say when a fight was bubbling up, "Go for what you know."

Acknowledgments

With great appreciation to the diligent and imaginative work of the Four Graces of Perseus Books: Vice President and Publisher Elizabeth "Big Time" Maguire, with whom this volume was conceived; my editor Megan "Happy" Hustad; Kay "You Can Count on Me" Mariea, Editorial Production Manager; and Chrisona Schmidt, perhaps the Western world's fastest Copy Editor.

Index